GARDENING THE SOUL

Gardening the Soul

A Spiritual Daybook
Through the Seasons

Sr Stanislaus Kennedy

1/490721

TownHouse

**SIMON &
SCHUSTER**

First published in Great Britain by Simon & Schuster/TownHouse, 2001
An imprint of Simon & Schuster UK Ltd and TownHouse and
CountryHouse Ltd, Dublin

Simon & Schuster UK is a Viacom Company

1 3 5 7 9 10 8 6 4 2

Simon & Schuster UK Ltd
Africa House
64–78 Kingsway
London WC2B 6AH
www.simonsays.co.uk

Simon & Schuster Australia
Sydney

TownHouse and CountryHouse Ltd
Trinity House
Charleston Road
Ranelagh
Dublin 6
Ireland

A CIP catalogue record for this book is available from the British Library

ISBN 1-903650-05-4

Typeset by Palimpsest Book Production Limited,
Polmont, Stirlingshire
Printed and bound in Great Britain by
The Bath Press, Bath

Author's Note
I am conscious that masculine pronouns dominate many of the
quotations but this is a reflection of the language used at the time and
not personal choice.

Introduction

These thoughts were written, not so much to find myself in print as simply to find myself, as they drew me more deeply into my inner journey with God and to God, and made me more attentive to my outward journey amidst the abundant beauty of creation and accompanied by so many wonderful people. It is my hope that this book will bring solace and comfort to all those who read it on their journeying.

I wish to express my appreciation and gratitude to Treasa Coady and all at TownHouse who encouraged me to write the book in the first place and continued to support and encourage me as I did so. A very special thanks to Siobhán Parkinson, who gave invaluable help with the text, and to the many people who typed different drafts of the book and especially to Síle Wall, who was involved with all the drafts. Finally I want to thank all those who have been a source of inspiration in my life and who are all in this book in one way or another, named or unnamed.

January/February

In solitude we learn to explore, and in still-ness we come to see that this is a time for new beginnings, a time to stop and be silent, to listen and to dream.

In January and February the garden grows in silence, the growth hidden from the gardener's view. There is hardly any colour, other than the browns and greys of soil and stone; there are no scents or sounds, no signs of life. But the gardener knows that there is plenty of invisible activity in the garden. Down under the soil, where the earth is warm even when frosts harden the ground, the roots are already preparing for spring, life is stirring in the depths. The gardener knows that in spite of the barren aspect of the garden, the spring bulbs are preparing to make their adventure to the world of light.

For the gardener, this is a time for planning and looking forward, for dreaming of possibilities and planning the summer garden. The gardener paces the garden in silence and in solitude, seeing what is not yet grown, dreaming of how the garden will look in the coming months, deciding what to put where, thinking about the seeds and the bulbs and their underground activity. This is a time for patience and for taking stock.

January and February call us to get in touch with the stillness of our own inner garden, to be patient with ourselves, to appreciate our inner strength and to embrace the seeds of beauty within us. In these months we learn to recognise the busyness of our daily lives, where silence may be a stranger.

Week 1

A winter garden is like the dark corners in our hearts which we try to ignore.

1 JANUARY

It is in the silent sanctuary of our own hearts that we make room for the transforming power of love to grow within us and radiate through us.

Allow your judgements their own silent undisturbed development, which like all progress must come from deep within and cannot be forced or hastened. Everything is gestation then birthing.

RAINER MARIA RILKE

2 JANUARY

We all need time to be ourselves. This does not mean differentiating ourselves as much as possible from others in style of dress, mannerisms or beliefs. Nor does it mean distinguishing ourselves in situations that require uniformity, such as in the army or in the corporate world. Rather, it means listening to our inner wisdom, identifying our uniqueness and marching to our own individual beat.

If a man does not keep pace with his companions perhaps it is because he hears a different drummer. Let him step to the music he hears, however measured or far away.

HENRY DAVID THOREAU

3 JANUARY

Even when we stop our bodies, our minds go on and on, racing and chattering, whether we are listening or not. The important thing is to *notice* the mind's chatter, for by noticing it we come to gain control over it and eventually to quieten it. It is not a question of judging it or thinking we shouldn't be having this internal chatter. The noise is there, but just noticing it will lessen its destructive effect.

Millions of people long for immortality who do not know what to do with themselves on a rainy afternoon.

SUSAN ERTZ

4 JANUARY

'*Ni h-é an t-éadaigh an fear* (clothes do not make the man).' This old Irish saying tells us, in no uncertain terms, that the things we possess do not and will not define us, nor bring us peace and happiness. Some may still believe abundant possessions bring happiness or that they are a sign of God's favour, but most of us know that when we are least reliant on material things, we are happiest.

A friend of mine who could be materially very well off made major changes in her home recently. By keeping only what she needed on a daily, weekly and monthly basis and giving away everything else, she has discovered the secret of living simply. This woman's attitude is a very simple one: people are more important than things. She has discovered that 'I have' is the greatest threat to who 'I am'.

I breathe in the green grass and in
The flowers, and in the living waters . . .
I permeate all things that they may
Not die, I am Life.

ST HILDEGARD OF BINGEN

5 JANUARY

In the stillness of silence, wisdom guides us to embrace those traits that previously were unknown to us, or that previously we weren't able to face. Meeting ourselves in this way can be disturbing, but once we accept and embrace ourselves, it brings us a peace and a calm we didn't know before – because we discover that, far from being as bad as we feared, we have a great beauty hidden within us, waiting to be explored.

Blessed is the man who, having nothing to say, abstains from giving us wordy evidence of the fact.

GEORGE ELIOT

6 JANUARY

If we listen, the earth can soothe our troubled hearts, refresh our weary limbs, soften our hardness and redirect us when we are lost. If we allow the sacredness of the earth to surprise us, we will not become withdrawn or sad or bitter or worn out; we will retain our vigour and our zest for life. The world will become for us an inexhaustible source of delight, of sounds, of textures, of colours, of patterns and harmonies. The world is a bottomless well, full of wonder and surprise, which can be endlessly drawn upon to recharge our spirits.

So rests the sky against the earth . . . I feel an ache of longing to share in this embrace, to be united and absorbed; a longing like carnal desire, but directed towards earth, water, sky and returned by the whispers of the trees, the fragrance of the soft soil, the caresses of the wind, the embrace of water and light. Content? No, no, no. But refreshed, rested while waiting.

DAG HAMMARSKJÖLD

7 JANUARY

Growing happens on its own. Most of the time we don't have to do anything. We just have to be present to ourselves and to others.

Caring is the same. It is not some special gift, the domain of rare individuals. The caring impulse is natural. It comes naturally to us, happens almost on its own, as long as we are aware of and respectful of others. Even the smallest, most ordinary act of kindness can reveal a glimpse of our divinity in our humanity, if it is done out of respect and love.

I grow in those seasons like corn in the night and they were far better than any work of the hands would have been.

HENRY DAVID THOREAU

Week 2

*Bareness and wildness in nature revitalises us
and refocuses our energy.*

8 JANUARY

To accept ourselves completely means, first of all, to
know ourselves – our shadowy, dark side as well as
our light, beautiful side – and to continue on the
road of discovering and knowing ourselves more
freely every day.

In order to do this, we need to care for ourselves
with the very same attention and open-heartedness
that we would like to offer others. Opening to our
own pain can be of immeasurable value in our efforts
to be of service to others, for as our understanding
of our own suffering deepens, we become more available to those we care for. Running away from our
pain limits us in our care for others.

The most terrifying thing is to accept oneself
completely.

CARL GUSTAV JUNG

9 JANUARY

A man who had lost his young wife in a tragic accident said to me once, 'I wish they would stop talking and trying to be helpful.' We all want to reach out to people in distress; there is a pull to fix things, to look for a solution. But maybe what the other person needs is not for us to talk but to listen. First, though, we need to calm the agitation of our own minds. If we develop a listening mind, we can become more centred, more focused, and in that way we can deepen our powers to heal and to help.

The way to do is to be.

LAO TZU

10 January

A life that is too busy, distracted and unfocused kills the power of imagination. If we cannot be still, if we cannot come to ourselves in silence, then we lose the power to imagine, and if we cannot imagine and dream, then we will never be able to realise what we desire.

Peace hath her victories
No less renowned than war.

JOHN MILTON

11 JANUARY

We are so used to an abundance of words that silence tends to frighten us. It seems to us like a vast empty space; we look down into its expanse and get dizzy or else we feel a marvellous attraction towards the silence that leaves us bewildered.

But when we discover silence, when we take the time each day, even if it is only for five or ten minutes, to close our eyes and to shut away the busyness of our lives, we find that this great emptiness of silence is already filled to the brim with what we cannot even imagine. Divine wisdom awaits us all in stillness and in silence.

After he had dismissed them, he went up on a mountainside by himself to pray. When evening came, he was there alone.

MATTHEW 14:23

12 JANUARY

As long as we go around unsurprised and taking things for granted, we never see the light. But in silence and stillness, wisdom opens to surprise. We arrive at an ability to wonder and to be surprised by being still within ourselves and responding to the gifts we are offered every day by the divine wisdom.

Real learning comes when the competitive spirit has ceased.

JIDDU KRISHNAMURTI

13 JANUARY

People sometimes confuse solitude with loneliness, but they are quite different. Loneliness is a painful experience that we feel when we are cut off or excluded, whereas solitude is an experience of being empty, free, serene and at peace, and yet alone.

Sometimes we need solitude so that we can confront our loneliness, and confront too the real cause of our loneliness. Perhaps we are lonely because there is something wrong in our lives; if that is the case, confronting our loneliness can help us to see this and may lead us to seek the appropriate help.

Or it may be that we are lonely simply because we have never rested with ourselves in solitude. To cope with our loneliness, it may be that rather than running out to find company we need to give ourselves up to the kind of solitude that allows us to deepen our sense of wonder.

Never less lonely than when completely alone.

CICERO

14 JANUARY

Silence and stillness are useless, in the sense that, like many of life's most important elements – water, air, the sea, mountains, flowers – we cannot assess their value in monetary terms. We have to learn their usefulness through our experience of our need for them. What is truly necessary will always crave our attention. 'Behold the lilies of the field': here Jesus is inviting us to take time to open ourselves to what appears to be useless, to see things as they really are, and to learn to value them.

We are all one silence in a diversity of voices.

THOMAS MERTON

Week 3

Perfectionism is the voice of the oppressor.

15 JANUARY

Openness is the ability to receive the gifts the world has to offer. Being open to the now means being receptive, with our hearts and minds, to whatever comes. We can only live fully and spontaneously if we have learned to be open to the now. The more present we are to the now, the more open we are, the more accepting we are and the less critical we are of ourselves and others.

For everything that lives is holy, life delights in life.

WILLIAM BLAKE

16 JANUARY

Rest is an interval in the busy rhythm of our lives. It renews and freshens us. It helps us to become clearer, stronger, life-giving people. A time of rest, a fallow time, prepares us for the next time, the time when we need to be about our business. Rest fills us with vigour and readiness for action as we go about living out who we are.

By the seventh day God had finished the work he had been doing; so on the seventh day he rested from all his work. And God blessed the seventh day and made it holy, because on it he rested from all the work of creating he had done.

GENESIS 2:2–3

17 JANUARY

A time to rest is a time simply to be. Time alone and at rest challenges us to confront the reality of our value as human beings, rather than as human doers. It allows us to hear the spirit speaking to us and it allows us to open ourselves to darkness as well as to light, to moments that are desolate, empty, lonely or confusing. In doing that, we embrace the possibility of hope, as the morning light spreads across a dark sky.

The Israelites are to observe the Sabbath, celebrating it for the generations to come as a lasting covenant. It will be a sign between me and the Israelites for ever, for in six days the Lord made the heavens and the earth, and on the seventh day he abstained from work and rested.

EXODUS 31:16–17

18 JANUARY

The Greek language distinguishes between *chronos,* which means measurable clock time, or calendar time, and *kairos,* which has a variety of meanings including the opportune or favourable time. *Kairos* can mean also a time that is made special and gracious by a sense of one's presence to oneself, to creation and to the creator; we can think of it as God's time.

Our age is obsessed with *chronos.* Our daily lives are ruled by schedules and it is a constant battle to keep things on time. But we need also to make room in our lives for *kairos,* or holy time. And to do that, we need to listen to the voice within us that is reminding us to stop, the voice that is trying to reveal to us when it is time to sow or to reap, to wait or to go.

Health requires this relaxation,
The aimless life,
This life in the present.

HENRY DAVID THOREAU

19 JANUARY

There are times when we think, like the poor widow who shared her last bread with the prophet Elijah, that we have nothing left to give. But it is often at these times that we find new resources in ourselves.

The same can happen with people we are trying to help. They may seem to have no education, no programme, no sermon, no sound advice, no solution to their problems. But what they have to give is important, and they give not from their surplus, but from their substance. We may find that they have offered us their very being, their presence, their hearts.

She went away and did as Elijah had told her so there was food everyday for Elijah and for the woman and her family. For the jar of flour was not used up and the jug of oil did not run dry, in keeping with the word of the Lord spoken by Elijah.

1 KINGS 17:15–16

20 JANUARY

Acknowledging our own weakness is an essential quality for those of us who work to provide a service to people who have been hurt and rejected. In situations where we are unable to be welcoming because we are just too tired or too busy, it is better that we acknowledge and accept that. People who have been repeatedly rejected see very clearly if there is a gap between what we say and what we do, between our ideals and our reality, and if they sense our hypocrisy, they will feel rejected and devalued once again.

It takes two to speak the truth, one to speak and another to hear.

HENRY DAVID THOREAU

21 JANUARY

City life is marked and scarred by the exploitative urban economy. I sometimes think that a return to a more rural way of life could be a source of renewal. But such a revolution would have to be accomplished by the community itself, not from outside by experts but from inside, based on the ancient rule of neighbourliness, the love of precious things and the wish to be at home.

Type of the wise who soar, but never roam;
True to the kindred points of Heaven and Home!

WILLIAM WORDSWORTH

Week 4

Gentleness is ungrudging and, like the winter soil, quietly facilitates growth.

22 JANUARY

It is difficult to take the risks that love demands of us; it is difficult to reveal our vulnerability. Living in a loving community with other people, however, living and working in a way that celebrates ourselves and each other, provides us with the support we need to enable us to take those risks.

There is no path to truth. Truth must be discovered but there is no formula for its discovery . . . you must get out on an uncharted sea and the uncharted sea is yourself.

JIDDU KRISHNAMURTI

23 JANUARY

Much of the time we live trapped inside a hectic, mechanical lifestyle, getting up to the sound of an alarm clock, battered by news from the radio, tested by traffic, forced to calculate time and distance to the minute, going through the day using phones and lifts and gadgets, then going home again at the end of the day, through more traffic, with more news being shouted at us.

It is only when we make time for silence and for prayer that we give ourselves a chance to remember who we really are and what life is really about.

The well of Providence is deep. It's the buckets we bring to it that are small.

MARY WEBB

24 JANUARY

We all have the seed of God in us, and it is because it is there, wanting to grow in us, that we cannot settle into complacency but must be always ready to grow. But we do not always allow ourselves to grow. We resist change, and that means we resist growing into our true selves.

The seed of God grows into God as a hazel seed grows into a hazel tree.

MEISTER ECKHART

25 JANUARY

Real intimacy leads into unknown territory, and we find our way only through trial and error. As we leave behind old, familiar ways of being, we move towards new states of balance. Falling into one extreme or another is unavoidable along the way. We must give ourselves permission to go overboard sometimes. If we attack ourselves for going off course, we cannot learn from our mistakes.

The softest things in the world overcome the hardest things in the world.

LAO TZU

26 JANUARY

Practising gentleness does not mean always liking what we see or simply tolerating whatever goes on in our relationships. But whatever arises, if we are gentle we can learn to be with it and let it be as it is. When we open to our experience as it is, without imposing blame, we start to make friends with ourselves. Only then can our defensive structure begin to relax, clearing the way for a larger wisdom to shine through for ourselves and for others.

The gentle minde by gentle deeds is knowne.

EDMUND SPENSER

27 JANUARY

Being people of courage and hope does not mean not feeling afraid; rather, courage is the willingness to stay open to our fear and our rawness, without running away.

None of us is courageous all the time. With fear we embark on most journeys. Courage appears when we are willing to sit at the edge of our pain and look at it face to face.

He that has light within his own cleer brest
may sit i' th' center, and enjoy bright day;
But he that hides a dark soul . . . Himself is
   his own dungeon.

JOHN MILTON

28 JANUARY

Eastern philosophy sees all life as the outcome of the harmonious synthesis of the two life forces of yin and yang, the power of quietness and the force of activity. We in the West, however, see these life forces as opposed, a matter of choice rather than a matter of harmony, and many of us choose yang over yin; quantity over quality; success over fruitfulness. And so we run ourselves into the ground, burning the candle at both ends to achieve targets, set mainly by other people.

You must learn to be still in the midst of activity and to be vibrantly alive in repose.

INDIRA GANDHI

Week 5

*The fruits of winter may be slow to ripen but
they are also slow to fall.*

29 JANUARY

Every living thing, other than the human being, is
capable of living in a balanced way, of balancing the
times of rest and activity, the times of light and darkness.

Each moment opens the wholeness of time.

POPE JOHN PAUL II

30 JANUARY

Imagine what it would be like if we were able to set boundaries to our lives that would prevent us from becoming worn and burnt out. Imagine what it would be like if we were setting the limits, rather than constantly forcing ourselves to respond to the limits set by others.

Imagine it, and then do it.

Spend the afternoon: you can't take it with you.

ANNIE DILLARD

31 JANUARY

With self-esteem, we cannot lose, no matter what we lose. When we have a sense of ourselves, no one can best us. Conversely, when we take away people's self-esteem then we have taken their all.

Those who respect themselves are safe from others. They wear a coat of mail that none can pierce.

HENRY WADSWORTH LONGFELLOW

1 FEBRUARY

We all enjoy a certain amount of stability in our lives: we relish the usual because it makes us feel secure. But sometimes we need variety too. Variety and change are good, so long as they are based on a core of certainty and stability. But if we do not have a stable core in our lives, our tendency to seek variety and change can confuse and upset us, and our lives can end up feeling rushed and chaotic. The secret is to find a balance between routine and variety.

You have many different natures, light and dark. Kind and mean. Inconsistent and predictable. You'll never be perfect. But you can be better than you are now. For your own sake, try.

NANCY WOOD

2 FEBRUARY

Some days, nothing seems to go right, and all we can hope for is that this miserable day will end. But regardless of how terrible our day may be, there is one thing that is always within our control: how we welcome, receive and complete each day is up to us. We can make the choice to change our attitude to what is happening to us, and that in turn affects everything the day brings, no matter how bad it may be. It isn't what we get each day that matters; it is what we do with it.

To affect the quality of the day, that is the highest of Arts.

HENRY DAVID THOREAU

3 FEBRUARY

We spend our days in a whirl of activity, often trying to do two things at the same time or thinking one thing and doing another. This is no way to live. Consider what nature expends to create even a single apple: it takes a spring, a summer and an autumn, and it takes blossom and bees and sunshine and rain. Anything that is forced or rushed is not whole. For anything worthwhile, even an apple, we need patience and time.

Tóg go bog é agus tiocfaidh sé chughat.
(Take things easy, and things will work out.)

A SAYING OF MY FATHER'S

4 FEBRUARY

Our lives are like the river that flows wherever it finds openings between cliffs and rocks, that finds a new course if the river is dammed or a cliff removed. And if things change in our lives – a new job, marriage, separation, a move to a new place – the river of life will simply take a different course. Like the river, we need to accept change in our lives and find a new direction. Otherwise our lives will never flow with ease.

The same stream of life
That runs through my veins
Night and day
Runs through the world
And dances in rhythmic measures.

RABINDRANATH TAGORE

Week 6

A seedling has its own rhythm; it emerges from rest and darkness only when its season has come.

5 FEBRUARY

Even though we know we have much to be grateful for and that we have achieved many things, we sometimes sense a vacuum in our lives and we search for something to fill it. But often what is missing is right there inside us. What has happened is that we have become separated from our true selves and the source of our being. When this happens, we need to stop, to listen to our inner voice, to become aware and attuned, to become truly awake.

Only that day dawns to which we are awake.

HENRY DAVID THOREAU

6 FEBRUARY

Acceptance of ourselves is the beginning of personal growth and transformation. In accepting ourselves, we face the fact of our own fragility and incompleteness, and it is by acknowledging that we are incomplete that we can change. Peace of mind is achieved not by filling in the gaps or correcting the flaws in our personality, but in understanding these flaws and accepting them as part of our reality.

God made everything out of nothing, but the nothing shows through.

PAUL VALÉRY

7 FEBRUARY

One of the great paradoxes of life is that it is through others that we can achieve self-knowledge, for true self-knowledge can be found only in the reflected appraisal of those whom we have loved and those who love us.

When people praise me for something
I vow with all my being
to return to my vegetable garden
and give credit where credit is due.

ROBERT AITKEN ROSHI

8 FEBRUARY

Spiritual energy is available to us if we learn to tap into it. That energy is released when we learn to notice: to smell the roses, taste the tea, notice the emotions in the eyes or the voice or the gestures of another. It helps us to harness these energies if we write down an account of them at the end of the day, to provide a source of energy that will inspire us tomorrow.

. . . looke in thy heart and write.

SIR PHILIP SIDNEY

9 FEBRUARY

The earth speaks in magic, but only to those who can hear with their hearts. Its voice is in the stark shape of a leafless twig against the winter sky, the touch of a water-worn stone, the colour of the sunset, the smell of the rain on the earth, the sound of the night wind. The earth's whispers are everywhere, but only those who have dreamt with the earth can hear them.

My soul can find no staircase to heaven unless it be through earth's loveliness.

MICHELANGELO

10 FEBRUARY

The pace of life has speeded up enormously, and this speed at which we are all living now has created a whole new set of problems. Perhaps the reason we feel so inadequate at times, so unable to cope, is that we are responding to new problems in old ways. New problems need new solutions, and new solutions require creativity and imagination. But first we need to notice that the problems have changed.

The dogmas of the quiet past are inadequate for the stormy present . . . as our case is new so we must think anew and act anew.

ABRAHAM LINCOLN

11 FEBRUARY

Sometimes we need to sit quietly and reflect in order to sustain our spirit, but this does not mean that spirituality is all about turning inward to attend to God and one's inner self. On the contrary, living a truly spiritual life is about living in the world with the conviction that God is to be found in everyone and everything. This conviction makes us engage with the world rather than turn away from it.

Clay is moulded into vessels and because of the space where there is nothing, you can carry water. Space is carved out from a wall, and because of the place where there is nothing, you can receive light. Be empty and you will remain full . . .

LAO TZU

Week 7

*In the desert of our lives we discover our own
poverty and our need for the Divine.*

12 FEBRUARY

Irish people sometimes use the expression 'she would
hear the grass growing'. Usually this is a derogatory
comment, meaning that the person referred to is
inquisitive and misses nothing. But to miss nothing
is a great gift. In order to notice, we have to take
the time to stop and listen and look. That's the only
way to hear the grass growing.

If we had a keen vision and feeling of all ordinary human life, it would be like hearing the grass
grow and the squirrel's heart beat and we should
die of that roar which lies on the other side of
the silence.

GEORGE ELIOT

13 FEBRUARY

Time out from the cares and anxieties of our everyday lives is something we all need, but, in order to take this time to be still with ourselves, we also need special places. You can use your bedroom or your workshop or your kitchen to take time out for prayer or meditation, but it's good also to have a place apart that you can visit, even if not every day – a place like a beach or a mountain walkway, a chapel or a quiet room, where you can feel truly at peace. Places apart are special because they give us space as well as time to reflect.

All the Goods of this world are finite and limited and radically incapable of satisfying the desire that perpetually burns within us for an infinite and perfect good.

SIMONE WEIL

16 FEBRUARY

Our defensive structures can only begin to relax and clear the way for a larger wisdom to shine through when we start to make friends with ourselves. And this can only happen when we are gentle with ourselves. We have to be gentle with ourselves before we can let gentleness flow out to others.

He makes me lie down in green pastures,
he leads me beside quiet waters,
he restores my soul.

PSALM 23:2

17 FEBRUARY

One morning I met a man coming out of an early-opening pub, clearly having been in for his 'cure'.

'Isn't it a great morning?' he said, more to himself than to me. 'I feel in great shape for the day.'

Each morning is a new opportunity to complete the day to the best of our ability. We don't all need a 'cure' to get us going in the morning, but we do all need to open ourselves up each morning to the day's possibilities and to greet the new day with enthusiasm.

God saw all that he had made, and it was very good.

GENESIS 1:31

18 FEBRUARY

Every new day is a gift we cannot produce for ourselves. The light comes and a whole new day is born, and it is different because of our reception of it. Even if the routine seems the same as yesterday, how we face today is always new.

Accept this world as Mount Sinai
Every moment we want manifestations
Every moment God manifests
And the mountain shatters.

RUMI

Week 8

As the stasis of winter nurtures plants and prepares them for growth, so silence and solitude nourish us and prepare us for adversity.

19 FEBRUARY

When we truly notice things, take note of their shape and smell and colour and form, they create resonant memories for us that we can carry with us to other occasions which are not so sweet or so hopeful.

Each of us must reach inside ourselves to find our own power sources.

SANDRA INGERMAN

20 FEBRUARY

I can remember a time when we had no television, no radio, no electricity even. We used candles and lamps for light, and at night the people used to tell each other stories.

Today we tell our stories to the people who are on chat shows or to our doctors or psychiatrists or solicitors, but not to our friends or neighbours for their entertainment. We have gained television, but, oh, what we have lost!

I have this potent prayer through good or ill:
here in the dark I clutch the garments of God.

JESSICA POWERS

21 FEBRUARY

People of good will often like to do things for others. We may feel better if we cook somebody a meal or buy them a gift or help them across the road. But often it is not action that the other person wants; what they want is for us simply to be with them. That is much more difficult, but much more precious.

Pearls lie not on the seashore. If thou desirest one, thou must dive for it.

ORIENTAL PROVERB

22 FEBRUARY

In the silent intimacy of solitude we discover our own uniqueness. In silence we can begin to hear the voice of our intuitive heart, a voice that is drowned in the noise of everyday living. But what is perhaps more surprising is that time alone in silence can dissolve the distance between us and other people and between us and the whole universe.

In the deserts of the heart
Let the healing fountain start . . .

W H AUDEN

23 FEBRUARY

Listening to the radio the other day I heard the programme's presenter ask a man who had rung in why he was phoning and where he was phoning from. He replied, 'Well, I am stuck here in traffic in Kinnegad and I have to be talking to someone or I would go mad.'

Ringing up a radio programme is one way of coping with the frustration of being stuck in traffic, but I find that carrying a Bible or a book of poems or a book of wise sayings and reading a line or two when the traffic is at a standstill is a great way to rise above the frustration.

Lord, what a busy restless thing hast thou made Man.

HENRY VAUGHAN

24 FEBRUARY

We are all precious in God's sight. Each of us has a unique role in the life of the universe, and this is our time and our place and no one else can take that time or place. No higher destiny is possible than to live our own lives, be in our own time, take up our own place.

The point of life is not to succeed
The point of life is to die trying.

EDNA ST VINCENT MILLAY

25 FEBRUARY

There is a widening gap between the consumerist values of individualism and the collectivist values of community. We can only fill this gap and make a positive, constructive difference by taking responsibility for our time and our society and by developing a sense of ownership of the world and times we live in.

Our minds are like crows. They pick up everything that glitters, no matter how uncomfortable our nests get with all that metal in them.

THOMAS MERTON

Week 9

We plan and plant our garden in hope,
accepting that while we can anticipate disasters
we cannot control them; for nature is controlled
by forces larger than we can comprehend.

26 FEBRUARY

God calls us forth, speaking to us before we were
born, before we are fully made in the womb of darkness. God takes us forth out of the night.

Sent forth by your senses God directs:
Go to the very edge of your longing and clothe
  me.

RAINER MARIA RILKE

27 FEBRUARY

Silence is demanding because it enables us to hear the chaos inside ourselves. As we come face to face with ourselves we come to recognise our own frailty and fragility, and so we are less quick to condemn others and less certain of our own convictions.

Life is a pure flame, and we live by an invisible sun within us.

THOMAS BROWNE

28 FEBRUARY

What I see, nobody else sees as I do. Because my vision is unique, how I see anything is mine and only mine. In that way I am a co-creator, completing what has already begun.

> To see a World in a Grain of Sand
> And a Heaven in a Wild Flower
> Hold Infinity in the palm of your hand
> And Eternity in an hour.

WILLIAM BLAKE

29 FEBRUARY

Everything depends on how attentive I am, how mindful I am of my unique opportunity to make this day, this morning, this person, this crocus, more beautiful, more whole, more complete because of my presence.

The happiness of a person resides in one thing – to be able to remain peacefully in a room.

BLAISE PASCAL

March/April

Hope *grows as life* emerges *from the darkness of the earth*.

After the long dark days of waiting, a miracle has happened. Yet again, perseverance has been rewarded; what has been hidden is now visible; our earlier attention to the invisible is being paid back with colourful surprises, one day after the other. It's brighter and lighter in the garden these days, with brighter mornings, longer evenings, cherry blossoms, birds in the trees, life budding into being – and it's lighter too in our hearts.

For the gardener, practical work begins in earnest now. Shovels, rakes and hoes are taken out of storage. The soil needs to be broken, aired and turned, tested for texture and food content. Plants that appear partly out of the ground need to be firmed back into place, while seedlings need to be planted outdoors in the places where they are to bloom.

March and April bring the season of Easter, with its time of waiting between Calvary and resurrection, between death and new life. The gift to pray for at this time of year is hope. We hope – we know – that the dawn of the year will come, with brighter days, fresh growth and colour in the garden. And yet hope is beyond what we imagine, because although spring always comes, it is always different.

1 MARCH

Spring is a time of change and openness to change. As life stirs in the garden, as the gardener gets to work, so our inner stirrings awaken us to our own potential for change and for growth. Our horizons are broadened, we can believe in the future, knowing that our lives will bring us all sorts of surprises as long as we leave space for new things to emerge, as long as we are open to the signs of the times.

If you trust the river of life, the river of life has an astonishing way of taking care of you.

JIDDU KRISHNAMURTI

2 MARCH

Trust in God, in the universe, is like entering into another realm of security; it is like diving into the sea with the dread of hitting the cold, but letting go anyway, diving anyway, and suddenly enjoying a new level of security as you swim under and between the waves.

> As swimmers dare
> to lie face to the sky
> and waters bear them
> as hawks rest upon air
> air sustains them.

DENISE LEVERTOV

3 MARCH

Some people love to take risks; they enjoy the thrill of it. Others fear risk. But whether we are natural risk-takers or not, we all have to live at times with uncertainty, insecurity, ambiguity – and for most of us that is not easy. What enables me to stay with the risk, comfortably or uncomfortably, is my trust that God's loving eyes are on me.

I will set my face to the wind
I will set my courage to keep on facing the wind.

ARABIAN PROVERB

Week 10

As the hidden bulb gradually brings forth the flower so, given time, our innate wisdom will develop what is authentic and good in us.

4 MARCH

Hope is not optimism. It is what we have when the bottom falls out of optimism. Hope is the ability to see through the false optimism of our time. It is the ability to see the reality of despair in the world and yet see that all is in tune with the divine purpose of creation.

In pursuit of knowledge,
every day something is acquired.
In pursuit of wisdom
every day something is dropped.

LAO TZU

5 MARCH

In everyday life, we can hope that our work will turn out all right, that the children will thrive, that we will have a good summer and a good harvest. These are all things we can imagine. True hope is different. It goes beyond the imaginable. True hope is divine. It is beyond our dreams, our expectations, our imagination. It is the call to be what is not yet.

Unseen bud's infinite hidden well
under snow and ice
under the darkness
in every square cubic inch
Germinal exquisite in delicate lace, microscopic,
    unborn
like babes in wombs, latent, folded, compact,
    sleeping
Billions of billions and trillions of trillions of them
    waiting
on earth and in the sea – the universe – the stars,
    the air in the heavens
urging slowly, surely, forward, forming, endless
and waiting even more forever more behind.

WALT WHITMAN

6 MARCH

When we take risks, when we let the props go and give ourselves up to the struggle, the goodness of God is more radiant than at other times.

What is love? I have met it on the streets, a weary poor man who was in love. His hat was old, his coat worn. The water passed through his shoes and the stars through his eyes.

VICTOR HUGO

7 MARCH

No matter how oppressed we may be, we always retain some capacity to choose. We can choose to risk ourselves to the goodness of God, or to continue to strive for our own autonomy, or to give in to the power that oppresses us. The choice is totally up to us. The sacred empowers us to choose rightly in what seems to be the most choiceless of situations, but it does not and will not determine that choice.

Then you will know the truth, and the truth will set you free.

JOHN 8:32

8 MARCH

The power of the sacred flows more fully when we choose to act in harmony with divine will. In practical terms, this means staying in a situation, being willing to confront it as it is, remaining responsible for the choices we make.

The art of medicine consists of amusing the patient while nature cures the disease.

VOLTAIRE

9 MARCH

Each day we grow older, but even as we age, we are in a constant state of growth. Growth comes through the decisions we make, the challenges we face, the people we meet, the risks we take, the setbacks we experience, the opportunities we take. How we grow depends on how we receive what comes to us.

With stammering lips and insufficient sound
I strive and struggle to deliver right the music of
    my nature.

ELIZABETH BARRETT BROWNING

10 MARCH

Each day is an exciting new step in our journey to maturity. We cannot reverse the natural progress of years, but no matter how old we are, there is always an opportunity, every day, for us to mature. All we have to do is to choose to take it.

In spite of that, we call this Friday good.

T S ELIOT

Week 11

The unfolding bud makes us aware of our unfolding selves.

11 MARCH

A young Indian shepherd boy spent a bitterly cold night lost on a mountain. Astonishingly, he returned to his family the next day, alive and safe. When they asked him how he survived he replied: 'When all the skies were dark, I saw far off another shepherd's fire on another mountain. I kept my eyes steadily on the red fire in the distance and I dreamed of being home.'

We all need a fire on another mountain to keep our hope alive on the nights when our struggles are dark and bitterly cold, but we must each discover that fire for ourselves. For each of us it is a different fire, a different dream, a different hope.

Act as if everything depended on you,
trust as if everything depended on God.

ST IGNATIUS OF LOYOLA

12 March

This is a story of Tolstoy's:

On his way to the Holy Land, an old person stopped at a house to ask for a drink of water; his companion, meanwhile, fell asleep under a tree. When the sleeper woke up, he assumed his friend had gone on ahead, so he boarded the boat and went to Jerusalem.

When he got to Jerusalem, he could see his friend in the temple, but then he missed him in the crowd. This happened twice more.

When he came home, the pilgrim discovered that his friend had not gone to Jerusalem at all. His friend had found that all the people in the house where he had asked for water were sick, so he had stayed to take care of them. The pilgrim could not help wondering which of them had reached his goal.

> We shall not cease from exploration
> And the end of all our exploring
> Will be to arrive where we started
> And know the place for the first time.

T S ELIOT

13 MARCH

Fear of not measuring up runs very deep. That's because we tend to live competitively instead of creatively. Competitiveness makes us lose not only our flow of inspiration, but even our courage and conviction too, and so we end up destroying and squandering our unique and precious gifts and talents by comparing them with others'.

Some people are so afraid to die they never begin to live.

HENRY VAN DYKE

14 MARCH

There is a creative tension between the now and the not yet. Sticking with the now can mean feeling settled once and for all, feeling that searching is a nuisance, feeling certain, and afraid of uncertainty. Following the not yet, on the other hand, may mean we go aimlessly searching all our lives, afraid of commitment.

Faith precedes hope. It takes faith to join the daring of the wanderer to the fear of the one who is satisfied in order to create hope.

Whatever you can do,
or dream, you can
begin it
Boldness has genius, power
And magic in it
Begin it now.

JOHANN WOLFGANG VON GOETHE

15 MARCH

Once when I was quite upset and uncertain about a situation in which I found myself – a situation over which I had neither control nor the possibility of rectification – feeling totally misunderstood and misrepresented, I read over and over again this passage from Jeremiah and prayed with it. It brought me great consolation and hope. I didn't know what it meant and didn't know what would happen, but I knew God had great plans for me. Even though I was full of uncertainty I was able to live with that uncertainty, knowing that God had a future full of hope for me.

'For I know the plans I have for you,' declares the Lord, 'plans to prosper you and not to harm you, plans to give you hope and a future.'

JEREMIAH 29:11

16 MARCH

To become a truly good person, we must be still, and face the loneliness and fear inside us. Waiting quietly allows us to listen to our own depths and to hear God's spirit there, yearning to bring us into maturity, to bring us into discovering ourselves and what is important in life.

This waiting can be heartbreaking. Nothing appears to be happening. But out of the heartbreaking darkness comes, slowly, the light.

Who can wait quietly until the mud settles?

LAO TZU

17 MARCH

To hope is to experience a power and a presence that is greater than we are, and to experience it when we do not see it. One way to experience what we do not see is to draw on memory, and especially on treasured memories of playful childhood moments. Such memories sustain prisoners in their captivity, and they can sustain us too.

No man and no force can abolish memory.

FRANKLIN D ROOSEVELT

Week 12

A miracle need not be a sudden event; we can perceive the miraculous in everyday experience.

18 MARCH

Many years ago I was involved in the introduction of a meals-on-wheels scheme for elderly people. Before the scheme was set up, people said there was no need for it, but as soon as we began to deliver meals they suddenly saw that indeed there were people who could not prepare meals for themselves.

One reason that people do not see situations as they are is because they are afraid that they will not be able to handle them. But if people are shown solutions, then they suddenly see the problem too.

Things do not change, we change.

HENRY DAVID THOREAU

19 MARCH

When the going gets tough those of us who are older often hark back to the 'good old days'. Of course, there was never such a time. There is no doubt that we can at times find comfort in the past, but there is also a danger that if we cling to the past we will only half-live in the present, half-experience the present moment. That is no way to honour the past. To honour the past, we must absorb its lessons and live them in the present.

Hope is about attending fully, to be without cleverness.
To be open to all things and to do nothing.

LAO TZU

20 MARCH

The poet Rilke was, at one time, employed by the great sculptor, Rodin. One day Rodin advised him to go down to the zoo to see something. Rilke spent hours watching a panther, and as a result of this experience he wrote nearly two hundred poems in an effort to sharpen his ability to see – to observe, to use the terrific energy of the eyes, to pay attention to something outside himself.

Not only artists and poets need to cultivate the ability to see. We all need to learn to get out of our own way, to see what is around us, and to see into the heart of others.

Not only is there but one way of *doing* things rightly, but there is only one way of *seeing* them, and that is, seeing the whole of them.

JOHN RUSKIN

21 MARCH

Hope is stubborn. It has the ability to accept strength and weakness. It is not arrogant; neither is it modest. Hope is daring, courageous; it has the audacity to reach a hand into darkness and come out with a handful of light.

> All will be well
> and all will be well
> and all will be well
> and all manner of things will be well.

JULIAN OF NORWICH

22 March

Waiting with a resilience of spirit, in the certain knowledge that, if we wait long enough and if we are true to ourselves, then things will make sense, is waiting in hope. And this is the work of the prophet – living in hope.

I said to my soul be still and wait without hope
For hope would be hope for the wrong thing;
    wait without love
For love would be love for the wrong thing; there
    is yet faith
But the faith and the love and the hope are all in
    the waiting.

T S ELIOT

23 MARCH

Hope lives on the edge between the near and the not far, between the infinite and the finite. It is believing what is not seen; it is seeing what is not visible; it is living as though the truth were true.

Hope is an orientation of the heart and spirit. It is not believing things will turn out well but the certainty that things will make sense no matter how they turn out.

VACLAV HAVEL

24 MARCH

Birds are messengers of hope, whether it is the majesty and grace of a swan on a lake; the extraordinary flight of the wild geese, organised and patterned as the birds make way for one another, waiting for a sick one to recover, and rotating the leadership of the flock; or just the homely drift of sparrows in the garden, twittering with the joy of spring.

He waited seven more days and again sent out the dove from the ark. When the dove returned to him in the evening there in its beak was a freshly plucked olive leaf! Then Noah knew that the water had receded from the earth.

GENESIS 8:10–11

Week 13

Every bud aspires to be a flower and every flower holds the promise of the fruit.

25 MARCH

People of hope feel with the rejected ones of society – people living with oppression and violence, anguish, abuse; people who are homeless, prostituted and unemployed. We feel their pain, their hurt, their anguish, and we are righteously angry on their behalf.

This anger gives us the courage to speak and act for truth and justice, to turn the system upside down and to work for a different kind of society, where all people can live in peace and justice.

Rich and poor have this in common: The Lord is the Maker of them all.

PROVERBS 22:2

26 MARCH

If we lose touch with our sources, we are in danger of losing hope. That is why it is so important to stay close to nature, to listen to how the trees and flowers, potatoes and hedges, shrubs and bulbs grow in silence.

Patience and time do more than force and rage.

JEAN DE LA FONTAINE

27 MARCH

I attended a workshop recently on entrepreneurial skills. I was amazed to find that these leaders of society, these business people, experts, politicians, were all agreed that a good entrepreneur needed to live with uncertainty, risk and ambiguity; to know how to wait; to live with questions and to allow questions to emerge; to be stubborn and flexible; to hold on to beliefs which appear at times to be inconsistent.

That's exactly what the spiritual value of hope is, only we don't call it an 'entrepreneurial skill'.

But if you have nothing at all to create, then perhaps you create yourself.

CARL GUSTAV JUNG

28 MARCH

Recently I spoke with somebody who had been wrongly accused of something very serious. She could not defend herself because the incident involved other people, but she told me that she was prepared to 'wait for the truth to unfold'.

Waiting for the truth to unfold is not easy in a world that expects quick results, easy answers. That is a form of hope that demands great courage as well as great patience and the ability to believe that in the end there will be no winners and losers, only the truth.

It is the heart that gives, the fingers just let go.

NIGERIAN PROVERB

29 MARCH

A school principal I know was extremely despondent about her school, because the teachers were not teaching in the way that she had taught.

It became clear, as we talked, that the children were happy and the teachers were working well together. It took me a while to persuade the principal that the problem lay in herself. She was unhappy because things were not being done her way, but as long as nobody was being hurt or damaged and the children were happy and developing and learning, then there was no problem.

Let us look at our shortcomings and leave other people's alone . . . There is no reason why we should expect everyone else to travel by our road.

TERESA OF AVILA

30 MARCH

To be ourselves is the most wonderful thing we can be in the world. To realise the capacity we have to be ourselves is the work of a lifetime. It is the one thing we each can do superbly well, and that nobody else can do.

Dad, isn't it amazing that I exist?

A SMALL CHILD TO HER FATHER

31 MARCH

When Jesus said to the blind man, 'What do you want me to do for you?' he replied without the slightest hesitation, 'I want my sight.' Jesus said, 'Your sight is restored.'

The blind man was prepared to receive. He was open to extraordinary possibility. He was open to the miracle of hope.

In all things, one receives only in accordance with what one has given.

HONORÉ DE BALZAC

Week 14

The needs of our intuitive hearts can be drowned by the preoccupations of our busy minds.

1 APRIL

Vision is the gift the artist brings to society. First the artist has to learn to see, to sharpen the sense of sight so that he or she can see into the very essence of things. Then, from this heightened visual sense, the artist has to develop the power to create new things, things that have not been there before.

There is an artist in all of us, waiting to come to life. Only I can see what I see as I see it, and the more effort I put into seeing, the more honestly and truly I see, the more possibilities I see, and the more creative I can become.

The painter draws with his eyes not with his hand, whatever he sees if he sees it clear, he can put it down.

MAURICE GROSSER

2 APRIL

Our lives can be predictable, dull and uninteresting at times. That's just the way it is. But if we focus on how boring and repetitive our daily life is, we will feel dull and lifeless and our garden will become choked with weeds and nothing will reach fruition.

If we focus instead on living wholeheartedly, if we let our roots grow deep into everything we do, then we can transcend the monotony of the constant round of our daily lives and transform it into ecstasy.

If you treat a man as he appears to be, you make him worse than he is. But if you treat a man as if he already were what he potentially could be, you make him what he should be.

JOHANN WOLFGANG VON GOETHE

3 APRIL

Nature has gentle moments: soft winds, sprinkling rain, warm sunshine, floating petals. But nature also has incredible power to harm and hurt: earthquakes, thunderstorms, floods, the constant cycle of predation and death, pain and disease.

When we learn to recognise that this power and this gentleness are part of the same nature, we can begin to face the paradox of our own potential for gentleness and destructive power too.

When you feel yourself part of nature
You will live in harmony.

TAO 13

4 April

Every day the sun rises and sets, tides ebb and flow. All these things happen whether or not we notice them, but when we take time to notice them, we are filled with wonder. Even to think that every snow-drop is different. Billions and billions of snowdrops that fall, every single one wonderful, looking so much alike and yet no two are the same.

Angels can fly because they take themselves lightly.

G K CHESTERTON

5 April

Pollution affects the air, the ground, the water, the fish, animals, fruit, vegetables. Acid rain, depletion of the ozone layer, global warming – is nature going mad?

But it is we who have changed everything. It is we who are destroying nature and it is destroying us only in return. Until we protect every little thing on earth, nature cannot protect us.

Teach your children what we have taught our children, that the earth is our mother.

CHIEF SEATTLE

6 APRIL

Wonder is all around us – the night sky, growth in the garden, a tree, a flower, a bird. We can find wonder right where we are in our rooms just by noticing.

But if we don't notice, we miss it. And when we've missed it, this moment, this flower, this cloud, it's gone.

But ask the animals, and they will teach you, or the birds of the air, and they will tell you.

JOB 12:7

7 APRIL

Nature teaches us that nothing lasts for ever and nothing ever continues as it began. This gives us the courage to seek solutions to our difficulties, the courage to get through any hard time, because we know that no matter how hard it may seem at any given moment, it will go away.

This grand show is eternal. It is always sunrise somewhere; the dew is never all dried at once; a shower is forever falling, and vapour is ever rising. Eternal sunrise; eternal sunset; eternal dawn; eternal glory and sea and continents and islands, each in its turn as the round earth rolls.

JOHN MUIR

Week 15

*Pondering the mystery of our being
makes space in our minds for wonder.*

8 APRIL

I knew a woman who was widowed at a young age.
She was left with three small children and a farm to
run. I asked her what she did when she heard the
news of her husband's imminent death. She said, 'I
put on my coat and walked through the fields. It
was spring and in those fields I found a new courage,
a new hope, and I was able to pray.'

If you find when things are very bad and you are
full of fear that you are too angry with God to pray,
sometimes it helps to turn, as this woman did, to
nature; for in nature we can often find the release
that renews hope.

> If you understand, things
> Are just as they are
> If you do not understand, things
> Are just as they are.

ZEN VERSE

9 April

As we move into the third millennium, we need a symbol of hope, an image that is capable of encompassing the great traditions of the past, the energy of the present and hopes for the future.

Could a woman with child be the symbol for the third millennium? For contained within her womb is all the richness of ancestral heritage, the unique, creative moment of conception and the infinite potential of the future.

A great and wondrous sign appeared in heaven: a woman clothed with the sun, with the moon under her feet and a crown of twelve stars on her head. She was pregnant and cried out in pain as she was about to give birth.

REVELATION 12:1–2

10 April

To Mary Magdalene, who was weeping in unbelief
at the tomb of Jesus, one word was spoken, her
name, 'Mary', and she believed. In the sound of His
voice saying her name, she recognised Jesus. In the
space between where all things touch and meet, a
word, one simple word, had the infinite potential to
unleash power for life to renew itself.

God's gifts put man's best dreams to shame.

ELIZABETH BARRETT BROWNING

11 APRIL

It is hard to believe that the earthquakes that rock our planet, bringing misery and disaster, can bring good news. Yet seismologists tell us that earthquakes are essential for the renewal of the earth. Through the energy released from the earth's fiery centre, the crust of the earth is broken, forming new land.

We need an attitude of faith to see that the Spirit is hovering over the chaos and that new life is coming forth.

Not only so, but we also rejoice in our sufferings, because we know that suffering produces perseverance; perseverance, character; and character, hope.

ROMANS 5:3–4

12 APRIL

It's hard to see a new vision in the darkness around us. We wonder what we have learned from the Holocaust, Nagasaki, Rwanda, Angola, Bosnia, Kosovo, Northern Ireland. What sense can we make of atrocities, massacres, horrors, hunger, famine, disease? How do they relate to God's providence or God's will?

But it is out of darkness that light comes.

Hope begins in the dark.

ANNE LAMOTT

13 APRIL

Foxford Woollen Mills was a fabulous, imaginative, innovative project in the west of Ireland, giving employment to a whole neighbourhood. In 1907, on 23 January, the mills burnt down. Next morning, Sr Bernard, an Irish Sister of Charity who had founded the mills, having prayed through the night, came out and said to the people, 'All disasters have a value. Now our mistakes are burnt and we can start anew.'

A bird does not sing because it has an answer; it sings because it has a song.

CHINESE PROVERB

14 APRIL

The future is an embryo growing within each human, and our creativity is the amniotic fluid in which the future is nurtured. We do not reveal what we are nurturing to others, and we wait in trust and do not abort the offspring.

The future is purchased by the present.

SAMUEL JOHNSON

Week 16

Nature teaches us to take ourselves lightly, we can fly only after the cocoon has been broken.

15 April

When we wait in hope, if we surrender to the waiting, time no longer pushes against us and we move gracefully in our waiting.

He that lives in hope danceth without music.

GEORGE HERBERT

16 APRIL

To bring our own personal creative power to birth, we must first each dare to imagine ourselves as a creative, fruitful person, a person precious and unique in God's sight and called by God to greatness.

Run a Walter Mitty movie in your head: see yourself doing the most creative things you can imagine. Then ask yourself, 'How much of that character can I actually be? How much could I comfortably be? How much could I dare to be? Who am I called to be?'

Be content with what you have;
Rejoice in the way things are,
When you realise there is nothing lacking,
the whole world belongs to you.

LAO TZU

17 APRIL

There is very little in our lives that we have full control over, even if we try. But we can control the way we think and our attitudes, and these can change everything.

What has been will be again,
what has been done will be done again;
there is nothing new under the sun.

ECCLESIASTES 1:9

18 APRIL

We can develop healthy attitudes by practice. If we have a hope-filled attitude in one instance, it becomes easier to adopt the same attitude on the next occasion. Just as a doubtful attitude sows seeds of doubt, a hope-filled attitude teaches others what to expect from us and sows the seeds of hope.

Jesus said what I say to you I
say to all, stay awake.

THICH NHAT HANH

19 APRIL

The great medieval German mystic and composer, St Hildegard of Bingen, measured the health and well-being of situations and people according to their faith, hope, love and their harmony with nature.

The air
with its penetrating strength,
characterises
the victorious banner that is trust.
It gives light
To the fire's flame
And sprinkles
The imagination of believers
With a dew of hope.

ST HILDEGARD OF BINGEN

20 APRIL

To truly see something, we must look at it for a long time. To look at the green and say, 'I have seen spring in these woods' is not enough.

We must *be* the thing we see, get to *know* the tree or the flower, look at its colour until its blueness or its yellowness becomes as real as a sound. We must enter into the small silences between the leaves and buds and blossoms and flowers. We must take our time and touch the very peace they come from.

If you are in love
Then why are you asleep?

KABIR

21 APRIL

When there is no room for miracle or mystery in our lives, when we are filled with anxiety about our problems and the necessity to find pragmatic solutions, our capacity for hope diminishes, because hope belongs to the realm of mystery.

There are only two ways to live your life. One is as though nothing is a miracle. The other as though everything is a miracle.

ALBERT EINSTEIN

Week 17

Thinning out young plants is necessary for a healthy crop. Thinning the clutter in our lives makes space for spiritual growth.

22 APRIL

This is the Good News: our lives are not trivia or defined by the problems we face.

Love and truth, suffering and death are not objective problems that we confront but experiences that develop us as we experience them. We are in them, not outside them; they transcend us and compel us to explore a larger world of interaction and exchange.

Great thoughts come directly from the heart.

VAUVENARGUES

23 APRIL

When we cease to believe in our dreams, we disconnect ourselves from the revitalising energy of our life force, which is love. Shutting the door on our dreams is like turning out the lights of love.

Faith consists in believing what reason does not believe . . . It is enough for a thing to be possible for it to be believed.

VOLTAIRE

24 APRIL

I spend some time each year in rural Ireland, walking in nature and being refreshed by it. But when I come back to the city, I am plunged again into a world where life does not follow steadfast natural patterns, outcomes are unsure, and poverty, illness, distress and exploitation are all around me.

And yet, even here, in the fragile people among whom I live, I find the bright fabric of hope, people who are able to be strong in spite of terrible experiences, and they in turn fill me with hope.

Sunday is like a piece of bright golden brocade lying in a pile of white muslin.

Y VUCHIDE

25 APRIL

If we nourish the spirit in silence, through meditation or prayer, we enable the spirit to unfold. As the spirit unfolds, we can grow to be our better and our truer selves.

Only the heart knows how to find what is precious.

FYODOR DOSTOYEVSKY

26 April

The word courage comes from *coeur*, the French for 'heart'. The essence of courage is being willing to feel our heart, to be present to the moment and to be open to the other, even when things are difficult or painful.

But it is not enough to be open. We must also be willing to extend ourselves, to face up squarely to experience and let it affect us, to wake up and confront what is actually happening, rather than just go along with old stories. This is true courage.

Opening our eyes may take a lifetime. Seeing, however, happens in a flash of lightning. Be vigilant.

CHINESE PROVERB

27 APRIL

I once saw a father being taught how to help his child, who was profoundly deaf, to learn. The father had to use toys to stimulate the child. He had to make a fool of himself, to become the child and become the toy. He found it very hard, but in the end, because of the patience of the teacher, he learnt how to do it.

We have to be prepared to make fools of ourselves if we want to get in touch with our children and share with them the wonder and the excitement of the world.

The beauty of the world is Christ's tender smile for us coming through matter.

SIMONE WEIL

28 APRIL

Belief is never far removed from unbelief. Love is never far from hate. Hope is only a short distance from doubt and joy lives side by side with tears.

The thirst after happiness is never extinguished in the heart of man.

JEAN JACQUES ROUSSEAU

Week 18

*The harmony of the garden reflects the eternal
peace that we long for.*

29 APRIL

Hope is being aware of our mortality and accepting
it. Hope is believing there is beauty and meaning in
our life right up to the last moment.
When we let go, hope expands.

God touches us with a touch that is Emptiness
and empties us.

THOMAS MERTON

30 APRIL

The other day, in the middle of the city, I saw a bit of a tree growing out of an old chimney on the building opposite me – extraordinary, and yet utterly ordinary.

We find beauty in the ordinary, and suddenly we realise that no thing, no person, is ordinary.

Let the earth bless the Lord
Everything that grows from the earth bless the Lord.

THE CANTICLE OF DANIEL 3:74

May/June

*These months bring great joy as the freshness
of spring gives way to the beauty of early
summer.*

A new beauty appears as the garden fills with colour. Flowers open, leaves unfurl and trees start to put on their full summer foliage. Each day brings something new, especially in the perennial beds, and the gardener is busy indeed, feeding, watering, staking, mowing and nurturing the lawn, and dealing with the abundance of weeds and the surge of life among the garden pests who have found a foothold for themselves in the warming earth.

If the gardener is not careful, there will scarcely be time to enjoy it all, there is so much to be done to keep pace with nature's summer abundance. It is important to take time between tasks simply to sit and wonder, to take a cup of tea or a cool summer drink out into the garden and just sit and stare and experience the beauty and the joy of it.

These months, with their long, busy days and languorous evenings, are the time to tune in also to the beauty of our lives and to discover the joy there is in loving with grateful hearts.

1 MAY

There is beauty everywhere, even amid ugliness, brutality and violence. The wild flowers, delicate but determined, that bloom in odd, ugly urban corners are one manifestation of it. What we might consider a weed in the garden we can enjoy elsewhere as nature's unofficial existence and an unexpected blessing.

What is a weed? A plant whose virtues have not yet been discovered.

RALPH WALDO EMERSON

2 MAY

We are for ever being wooed into the wonder of God. There is deep in each of us a longing to be totally immersed in the eternal harmony and beauty of the world, and it is that longing that woos us into wonder.

Wonder will never be lacking in this world.
What is lacking is wonderment.

G K CHESTERTON

3 May

A young monk went to visit a highly regarded old monk in the desert, to ask him for a recipe to preserve his inner peace. To his great surprise, the old monk told him, 'I have worn the habit for seventy years and not in a single day have I found peace.'

Peace is not a possession or an achievement, but lies in an untiring striving after peace.

Only one feat is possible – not to have run away.

DAG HAMMARSKJÖLD

4 MAY

When we recognise beauty in the world, even if it is
only for a fleeting moment, it puts us in touch also
with the wonder of ourselves, 'the wonder of our
being', as the psalm says, and in that wonder we
find joy.

Little flower – but if I could understand
What you are root and all in ALL
I should know what God and man is.

ALFRED TENNYSON

5 MAY

Loving ourselves – not being preoccupied with ourselves, not forcing our personal selves to the centre of every experience, but healthy self-love – is necessary if we are to move out to others in love. People who have never learnt to value themselves will not have a source of security, serenity, joy and compassion for others to tap into.

In art as in life, anything is possible so long as it is done with love.

MARC CHAGALL

Week 19

There is beauty in a weed if we take time to look closely at it

6 MAY

We don't have to be able to do everything. We don't have to know everything. We don't have to be fast and efficient. We don't have to win, or even to take part in the race.

What we do have to be is ourselves, what we were created to be. What we do have to know is what our own gift is. What we have to do is to reach out with joy in love.

O Lord, you have searched me and you know me.
For you created my inmost being;
You knit me together in my mother's womb.

PSALM 139:1,13

7 MAY

Every beautiful thing we see mirrors the essence of God. Each one is a vessel filled with the manifestations of the creator.

Never lose an opportunity of
Seeing anything that is beautiful,
For beauty is God's handwriting,
A way-side sacrament.

RALPH WALDO EMERSON

8 MAY

Joy can never be an expected outcome of our hard work, our searching, our struggling. There's much that we can expect to gain from our own efforts – financial security, intellectual satisfaction, applause – but joy cannot be gained by work or effort.

For joy is a gift. Search for it, and you won't find it. Pray for it and it will come to you.

He who kisses the joy as it flies
lives in eternity's sunrise.

WILLIAM BLAKE

9 MAY

Loving is risky. To love is to be vulnerable. Giving your heart to someone ensures that it will be broken, pierced, wounded and made malleable. Give it anyway.

If you give your heart to no one it will become unbreakable, impenetrable, irredeemable.

C S LEWIS

10 MAY

Sometimes love is not enough. Indeed, love without skill and knowledge can be a hindrance, if the person we are caring for or trying to help is deeply wounded – by violence, abuse or depression, for example – and needs professional help.

The messages of such people are very often sent to us through difficult, disturbing behaviour. It takes professional skill to receive and decode these messages, and it is an essential part of caring to be able to recognise when outside help is needed.

Fear not, for I have redeemed you.

ISAIAH 43:1

11 MAY

We all know that the earth's resources are limited, and yet we act as if they were limitless. We nurture the naïve wish that the people of underdeveloped countries could enjoy the same standard of living as we do, but if they did, it would bring disaster, in terms of energy consumption, depletion of natural resources, pollution and waste generation – it is just not possible.

What a man had rather were true he more readily believes.

FRANCIS BACON

12 MAY

Love is our raison d'être. It is what we are made for as human beings. The human heart is made for praise, thanksgiving and love. This singular command is engraved in our hearts, and whether we understand this or not matters little; whether we agree or disagree makes no difference. For our only joy is in loving with a full heart.

Thou hast made me for thyself O Lord and my heart will never rest until it rests in thee.

ST AUGUSTINE

Week 20

The beauty of the rose and the splendour of the lily do not detract from the perfume of the sweet pea or the charm of a daisy.

13 MAY

I live as part of a small community of people from different backgrounds and traditions, and sometimes it is difficult to be so exposed, to be made to face every day one's own weaknesses and failings. But community – whether a religious community, a family or any group of people living or working together – is a loving environment, and in a loving environment we open our gifts each day to each other.

When you live for your soul, even without understanding this, you improve your social life.

LEO TOLSTOY

14 MAY

As parents, educators and teachers, our vision of the cosmos as God's creation, and not as humanity's warehouse or playground, challenges the individualism, utilitarianism and greed of the Western world's attitude to nature.

> With an eye made quiet by the power
> Of harmony, and the deep power of joy,
> We see into the life of things.

WILLIAM WORDSWORTH

15 MAY

Even the predictable can be wonderful if we wake up and stop taking it for granted. If we were fully awake, everything would be predictable and yet everything would be full of wonder. If we knew all about how our world worked, we would still wonder that the world existed at all.

Don't sit on the porch.
Go out and walk in the rain.

KABIR

16 MAY

We learn who we are from the way others acknowledge, accept, appreciate and believe in us. When we are acknowledged and affirmed, our confidence grows. When we are accepted in spite of our limitations, we learn to see those limitations in perspective and not to hate ourselves for them, but rather to rise above them.

Our challenge is to love others into living to their full potential, into growing to their full beauty.

Kind people help each other even without noticing, and evil people act against each other on purpose.

CHINESE PROVERB

17 MAY

The only gift that is greater than beauty is our awareness of it. Nature opens windows of wonder to us
daily, but it is up to us to notice the windows and
to look through them. If we do that, we live each
day against a collage of wonder.

Only beauty will save the world.

FYODOR DOSTOYEVSKY

18 MAY

It is easy to convince other people that they are ugly;
by our disdain, we can make them want to hide their
faces. Or we can look on them with love and reveal
to them their true value and beauty.

Jesus looked at him and loved him.

MARK 10:12

19 MAY

On the afternoon of 1 May 1998, I was driving to Dublin from Sligo. I had a wonderful view of the Curlew Mountains, with the sun shimmering on lake water, when I spotted a magnificent sculpture of a man on horseback looking down at me. I thought it was real, initially – I had to slow down to get a good look. Just at that moment Placido Domingo was singing one of my favourite pieces of Puccini on my car radio. A moment of sheer, unplanned joy.

But headlong joy is ever on the wing.

JOHN MILTON

Week 21

The seeds of beauty, goodness and truth lie within us. Though often unacknowledged, they are the seeds from which we grow to be strong, beautiful people.

20 MAY

The people who love us can love us into love, if we let them.

Love conquers all: let us also yield to love.

VIRGIL

21 MAY

When our life is filled with the desire to see the wonder in everyday life something magical happens: ordinary life becomes extraordinary.

Dance my heart,
Dance today with joy!

KABIR

22 MAY

Joy is playful: it is squirrels playing. Joy is light-hearted: it is ducks paddling on the pond. Joy is lively: it is a stream racing down the side of a hill, spinning over the rocks. Joy is at one with the moment: it is a cat stretching in a patch of sunlight, or a bee buzzing around the flowers.

Dear God, dear stars, dear trees, dear sky, dear people, dear everything, Dear God.

ALICE WALKER

23 MAY

When we live or work closely with people, each person's failings and weaknesses are exposed to the others. With this awareness of the frailty of others, there comes a choice: we can complain about and judge the other person or we can love them. Which brings more joy?

A friend is one to whom one pours out all the contents of one's heart – chaff and grain together, knowing that the gentlest hands will take and sift it, keep what is worth keeping, and with the breath of kindness blow the rest away.

ARABIAN PROVERB

24 MAY

The more we invest in our own privacy, the more we build walls around ourselves – psychological, physical, cultural and spiritual walls – the less able we are to see people as people.

Give all to love
Obey thy heart . . .
Nothing refuse.

RALPH WALDO EMERSON

25 MAY

Beneath every failure to love is fear – the conviction that it is not safe to give. But if we follow the way of fear we will become isolated and lonely, whereas when we follow the way of love it will lead to trust, community, friendship, transformation.

Real friendship is a slow grower and never thrives unless engrafted upon a stick of known and reciprocal merit.

G K CHESTERTON

26 MAY

Joy is in the overflow. Our society stays affluent by making its container bigger when it is just about to overflow, so the joy of overflowing is taken away. But if we make our vessel smaller and smaller, by reducing our needs, then the overflowing joy will come sooner and sooner.

On with the dance! Let joy be unconfined.

LORD BYRON

Week 22

The more hectic our lives, the more willing we are to trade beauty and happiness for success and desire and the less we are able to discern the difference between the two.

27 MAY

Joy does not depend on what happens. We can have joy no matter what happens, because joy stems from the core of our being – it is a gift. It is our whole-hearted response to whatever comes to us in any moment.

Burst into songs of joy together,
you ruins of Jerusalem.
for the Lord has comforted his people,
he has redeemed Jerusalem.

ISAIAH 52:9

28 May

On one of my first visits to the US, I was advised never to look the homeless people on the streets in the eye. Now, the one thing I know about homeless people is that their deepest need is to be recognised, to be greeted, to be shown respect, to be treated like 'ordinary' people. That is more important to them than food or clothes or shelter or money.

That was one piece of advice I didn't take.

Oblige with all your soul
The friend who has made
A present of his own.

SOCRATES

29 MAY

I once watched a long queue of women and children waiting to drop their buckets down into a very deep well in Nigeria. Towards the end, all the buckets weren't filled, but they shared what they had between them, and their joy was terrific.

How long must I remain in jeopardy
Of blank amazement and amaze no more.

JOHN KEATS

30 MAY

To find beauty and joy in the world around us, we only have to open our hearts and minds to the gratuitousness of everything in the world. When we do this, our spontaneous response is wonder, surprise and gratitude.

It happens. We don't have to strive for it.

The wise person does not strive
The ignorant man ties himself up
If you work on your mind
With your mind
How can you avoid an immense confusion?

SENG-TS'AN

31 MAY

Sometimes an overcrowded schedule and an over-loaded agenda can be a symptom of fear. We are running around, always trying to please people, always angry because too much is expected of us. We are angry on the surface, but underneath we are afraid – afraid to stop, to slow our wretched pace, to confront ourselves. We are afraid we mightn't be loved enough.

At the touch of love everyone becomes a poet.

PLATO

1 JUNE

Unconditional love offers the beloved roots and wings: roots give a sense of self and identity, and wings give a sense of independence and freedom.

But there is a space in between the roots and the wings, and across this space encouragement comes – empowering others to believe in themselves, the challenge towards transcendence, the awareness of the responsibility to heal and to redeem. When we understand this, we understand our own preciousness and blessedness.

My command is this: Love each other as I have loved you.

JOHN 15:12

2 June

On the eve of Pentecost, I called to visit our sisters in Cork. I arrived a little early and I went to visit the chapel. An elderly sister was preparing the altar. She moved each plant backwards, forwards, to the left, to the right, until all the plants were in their places. Then came the flowers, all different, all splendid. Again she moved them from place to place, and with each movement she stepped back to see her work in perspective. Each plant, flower, candle was arranged, placed with such deliberation, such respect, such gentleness, such love and care. Each had its own place and each added to and gained from the beauty of the other. When she had finished the altar was beautiful. I could not help thinking that if only we touched everything and everyone with the same respect and love that this sister showed for the plants and flowers, what a beautiful world we would have.

O body swayed to music, O brightening glance,
How can we know the dancer from the dance?

W B YEATS

Week 23

When we become aware of the beauty we are grateful for everything. Without this awareness we can become frantic and relentless in our demands.

3 JUNE

Jean Vanier once shared with me his thoughts on the statue in Chartres Cathedral of God creating Adam: 'God is gently drawing Adam out of the mud and Adam is resting on the breast of God . . . It is as if the artist was saying, "I love you, you are beautiful".'

Our task is to hear God saying to us each day: 'I have chosen you and you are precious and you are beautiful and I love you.'

For we are God's workmanship, created in Christ Jesus to do good works, which God prepared in advance for us to do.

EPHESIANS 2:10

4 JUNE

When we acknowledge our need to love or be loved we risk laying bare our vulnerable self. Some of us may never acknowledge our need for love, to protect our vulnerability.

But if we do not acknowledge our need, we will never get what we need. And so we have no choice but to risk getting the wrong response rather than getting no response at all.

Love cannot distrust.

MEISTER ECKHART

5 JUNE

We live in one another's company for a reason. Each one of us has unique gifts, but our gifts can be a burden if they are not shared. Our own growth and development depend partly on the contributions of others. We live better when we share in the presence and talents of others, just as others benefit from our positive involvement in their lives.

We are shaped and fashioned by what we love.

JOHANN WOLFGANG VON GOETHE

6 JUNE

Where there is love, the harshness of experience is softened. Whether we are the recipients of love or the givers, we benefit because in the giving and receiving we know we belong, and that is a deep, deep need in all of us.

Love is a high inducement to the individual to ripen, to become something in himself, to become a world to himself for another's sake.

RAINER MARIA RILKE

7 JUNE

'Say good morning to our new kitten,' said my six-year-old cousin, Colm, pushing the nose of the furry kitten up against my face while I was having my breakfast. He saw that I had not noticed the kitten. He was giving me a clear message.

When we are not noticing what is around us, we are blind to beauty; it has no magic for us; we are not fully alive; and, very quickly, cynicism can replace our sense of surprise.

Give ear and come to me;
hear me, that your soul may live.

ISAIAH 55:3

8 JUNE

God's love is always waiting, gently urging, assisting, longing, loving us into what we are called to be. We are God's summer roses.

Now to him who is able to do immeasurably more than all we ask or imagine, according to his power that is at work within us, to him be glory in the church and in Christ Jesus throughout all generations, for ever and ever! Amen.

EPHESIANS 3:20–21

9 JUNE

All we are asked to do is to love. That is all Christ
asked his followers to do. Yet it is the one thing we
find most difficult to do. Maybe it is because we rely
so much on our human efforts. If we see ourselves
as expressions of God's love, instruments of God's
love, it will become easier for us to love.

You are in the world only to love.

BLAISE PASCAL

Week 24

An appreciation of what is beautiful develops through time and reflection and enables us to be surprised by the sunset, and the kind word.

10 JUNE

When two people take the trouble to establish and maintain a friendship, they reveal themselves to each other in trust. The depth of the trust between them will determine the strength of their bond.

Among the elements constituting this friendly bond are generosity, the willingness to listen, the ability to respond, mutual acceptance of trust and mutual self-disclosure.

Partnership is a single soul dwelling in two bodies.

ARISTOTLE

11 JUNE

The more we love, the more loving we become. Love fosters kindness; love elicits respect; love clears the way for a positive attitude; love inspires hope and confidence; love brings joy, peace, beauty and harmony.

Love has a bunch of keys under its arm
Come, open the doors.

RUMI

12 JUNE

True love is not possessive. It leaves us free – free to receive it or not, to respond to it or not. It is humble, willing to perform the humblest of tasks to meet the other's needs. It is sensitive to the other's gifts, needs and aspirations. It is compassionate and generous and self-sacrificing. It leaves the other free to be him- or herself.

Love does not have to be earned: it is there for us, whether we respond to it or not.

Love wants to own nothing. It only wants to love.

HERMANN HESSE

13 JUNE

What we send out we get back. We can be certain that whatever we meet this day has its roots in our own past. Each loving response we make sets in motion new loving activities, which in time will find their way back to us.

Our deeds still travel with us from afar
And what we have been makes us what we are.

GEORGE ELIOT

14 June

Joan lived in our community for six years and we loved her. All her life, Joan had experienced rejection and exploitation and horrendous, unbelievable cruelty. But through it all she carried a spark of hope. Her spark sometimes flickered but it never went out.

'Will you come to my funeral, Stan?' she would ask. Then she'd laugh: 'Sure what would an oul' wan like you be doing at my funeral? You'll be well gone before me, with God's help.'

A stolen car driven on the wrong side of the road hit a pole which fell on Joan and killed her instantly. She was 49.

Joan owned nothing. Her apartment, though, was papered with all the cards she had received in her life.

All she had ever wanted was to be loved.

A thing of beauty is a joy forever:
Its loveliness increases; it will never
Pass into nothingness.

JOHN KEATS

15 JUNE

Creativity is a way of living that is open to us all, because it arises from the spirit within us. This is one of the best-kept secrets in the Western world. In fact, we have been taught the opposite: that creativity is only for the elitist few.

Of course there are in every generation some very specially talented artists, whose work brings great pleasure and joy. But if we put these great artists on a pedestal, to the exclusion of everyone else, we can kill off the creative gifts in the rest of us. And if we do that, we destroy our vitality as a people.

Not every artist is a special kind of person but every person is a special kind of artist.

ERIC GILL

16 JUNE

When we feel the pain of the constriction between the perfect love in our hearts and the obstacles to its complete realisation, it breaks our heart. When the heart breaks open we hurt, and in this pain we feel raw and tender – but we are, at that point, in touch with the very essence of who we are.

I have known shadow
I have known sun
And now I know
These two are one.

RUDYARD KIPLING

Week 25

Many beautiful things in life are too expensive for most of us to buy, but the beauty of creation is there for all of us, free for the taking.

17 JUNE

We always know in our heart of hearts what is best for us, but often we don't want to hear it and so we don't listen to it. Our heads tell us we're too busy even to think about taking a break, for example, even though our heart is crying out for us to take it easy.

That happened to me. I ignored my heart's pleading, until one day I got so sick with tiredness that I had to stop everything. That was a hard lesson. There is an easier way: if we consult with our inner selves and listen to our heart of hearts, there we will find the source of wisdom.

I lean and loaf at my ease . . . observing a spear of summer grass.

WALT WHITMAN

18 JUNE

If our experience of love has always been with conditions (I'll support you if you agree with my plan, I'll love you if you do what I want you to do, I'll be with you as long as it doesn't interfere with my life or my plans), then it is difficult for us to comprehend a faithful love that is not conditional – but such is the love of God.

O my Strength, I watch for you;
you, O God, are my fortress,
my loving God.

PSALM 59:9–10

19 JUNE

Love is about living with an open heart. It's about welcoming people, giving them a place in our hearts. It isn't about offering a limited service to one person and then moving on to the next. It is about opening our hearts and carrying people in our hearts, even at the times when we cannot give them the help they need.

. . . the heart that has truly loved never forgets.
But as truly loves on to the close . . .

THOMAS MOORE

20 JUNE

I was nearly drowned about fifteen years ago, and I still remember it as vividly as if it was yesterday – the struggle, the terror, the sheer desperate effort to survive.

It need not take an incident like this to make us aware of the importance of our bodies to us, and the lengths to which we are prepared to go, when our bodies are under attack, to stay alive. That will to live is one of God's hidden graces, a gift that helps us to survive in the struggle of life.

Your body is a city that is full of good and evil; you are King or Queen of this city and your heart is your best councillor.

EASTERN PROVERB

21 JUNE

I know a couple who devoted themselves untiringly and with extraordinary fidelity to their disabled child. They cared for him day and night, but after two years he died unexpectedly. They then had another child and they lavished the same faithful love and attention on her, but she got meningitis and also died, very suddenly. Then they adopted another child, who was cherished and loved as dearly as the others.

Faithfulness is not easy, but it is possible.

The kinder and more intelligent a person is, the more kindness he can find in others.

LEO TOLSTOY

22 JUNE

People who are in need – damaged, vulnerable, abused people – are afraid of revealing themselves and opening up to those who are trying to help them. They need people who will listen to them, with all their wounds and needs. They need to sense that they are not being judged. They need people who will help them to rediscover their self-esteem, self-respect, pride, dignity and sense of empowerment. Most of all they need acceptance.

The greatest blessing is a pleasant friend.

HORACE

23 JUNE

To love is to say Yes to belonging. When we fall in love our sense of belonging is overpowering, our Yes is bliss. But when things are difficult and stressful it may be more difficult to say Yes.

To know we belong in both the good and the bad times is to know love in our heart of hearts.

Dear friends, let us love one another, for love comes from God. Everyone who loves has been born of God and knows God.

1 JOHN 4:7

Week 26

There is delight in the gardener's face as he digs up his first new potatoes.

24 JUNE

Faithfulness is a special way of loving that mirrors the fidelity of God's unconditional love. But we cannot be faithful in a destructive or abusive situation, where the loved one is destroying us and preventing us from growing in love. This does not mean that we are faithless, but that the person or situation we love is rejecting our love.

We can try to stay with the situation, out of obligation or duty, but that is not fidelity, for true fidelity is life-giving, and sticking with an abusive situation is life-destroying.

Our fullest humanity is God's glory.

ST IRENIUS

25 June

When our heart breaks out of its protective shell, we shed our ideal images of how we should be and we feel naked. It is in this nakedness that we taste the essential nature of our existence, and we are healed.

There is nothing in which real wisdom cannot be displayed.

LEO TOLSTOY

26 June

We all have glimpses from time to time of our mission in life, a vision of our special gift. But most of the time our hearts are too closed, too clouded to capture the vision God has for us.

But even if we close our hearts, God draws us ceaselessly to himself, and that is what accounts for our restlessness, or half-acknowledged desire for another way of being, for a place where our spirits are nourished, another land where our souls are free.

We must be willing to get rid of the life we've planned so as to have the life that is waiting for us.

JOSEPH CAMPBELL

27 June

We are all part of God's dream and God dreams in us. Not everyone is comfortable with the word 'God', but the power that dreams in us is the power that calls us forth to our full potential, to realise the dream.

It is never too late to be what you might have been.

GEORGE ELIOT

28 JUNE

Christ's command to love is really very simple, but we have great difficulty with it. It means that our true self is not just our ego, but it expands also to include our neighbour.

It costs us no effort to belong to ourselves – we automatically, spontaneously, say Yes to ourselves in our hearts. But love means that we say Yes also from our heart to our true self, to our neighbour, and that we live accordingly.

You can't work with people without love, just as you cannot work with bees without caution. If you are not very cautious with bees you harm both yourself and the bees. The same happens with people. Mutual love is the highest law of our existence.

LEO TOLSTOY

29 JUNE

If we believe we are created in love and out of love and that we live in the great divine love, then we believe that every time we love, the ramification of that act of love is infinitely greater than anything we can ask or imagine.

We are creators of the world around us by our every act of love. No loving thought, word or action escapes the ripple effect.

It's a funny thing about life; if you refuse to settle for anything less than the best, that's what it will give you.

W SOMERSET MAUGHAM

30 JUNE

True acceptance and welcome are found not only in the great unusual moments when we have a lively sense of being loved fully; they are equally present in the small gestures of tenderness, forgiveness and humility that are part of everyday life.

Surely the Lord is in this place, and I was not aware of it.

GENESIS 28:16

July/August

The fullness *of the garden in high summer is a* blessing *for the soul.*

This is a season that is generous with its delights. The garden is lush with growth and bright with flowers – the borders are a rainbow of colour, the hanging baskets full to overflowing, the sweet peas scented and exquisite. We have a foretaste of harvest as we enjoy the scents of summer and pick our raspberries and plums.

At this time of year, we are at our busiest in the garden. Roses need to be sprayed, gaps in the perennial border need to be filled out with annuals, flowers need to be dead-headed to encourage a new spurt of growth, cuttings need to be taken.

So much to do – and yet, if we spend all our time doing it, we won't get any time to enjoy it. If we can remind ourselves to slow down and just look, then the fullness of the summer garden fills us with gratitude and we cannot help but give praise and thanksgiving and blessing.

To bless is to honour, to honour is to celebrate, to celebrate is to experience joy and to experience joy is to give thanks.

Week 27

*Falling apple blossom reveals the
burgeoning fruit.*

1 JULY

At this time of year, we hope for good, sunny weather
so that it will be warm enough to sit in the garden
and really enjoy it. We need these lazy afternoons in
the sunshine; we need to treat ourselves, to love
ourselves, to give ourselves a rest. Because unless we
start loving ourselves and realising our own
preciousness, we are wasting our lives. It is as serious
as that.

Our desire is not that others might be relieved
while you are hard pressed, but that there might
be equality.

2 CORINTHIANS 8:13

2 July

'Good luck, girl, *agus go mbeannaí Dia thú*,' was how my father always said goodbye to us, each time we left home. At the time, I didn't notice it, but now I realise that when he said those words, he would raise his hand, in a gesture of blessing. My mother did it differently: she blessed us with holy water as we went to bed as children, and every time we left home she blessed us in the same way, and she did it until she died, much to our embarrassment as teenagers.

Formal blessings are rare in our society now (apart from in church) but parents do it all the time to their children – laying a hand on their head or shoulder, wishing them well. A lovely custom, and one we might remember and enact more consciously.

But just as the capacity to forget is a gift of grace, so memory, the recalling of lessons we have learnt, is also part of responsible living.

DIETRICH BONHOEFFER

3 JULY

If we are to be ourselves we must be true to our inner wisdom and live according to our own rhythm, not according to the clock or the calendar or somebody else's agenda.

We must learn to listen to the music of this moment, to hear its sweet implorings and sober directives. We must learn to dance a little in our hearts, to open our inner gates a little more. That is how we tune in to the divine wisdom, the breath of the universe.

Wisdom is the breath of the power of God.

WISDOM 7:25

4 JULY

Even the smallest particle of creation is a revelation of God, but we need to see with the eyes of the heart if we are to read the wind, the sand, the stars, people, beneath the first level of appearance.

There are surprises and special gifts to help us all make this transition, from the eyes in our head to the eyes of our heart. If we spend time contemplating anything it is transformed – every weed becomes a flower, every grey morning an awakening, every wave of the ocean the heartbeat of the universe – and we get a glimpse of the divine.

For I greet him the days I meet him, and bless when I understand.

GERALD MANLEY HOPKINS

5 JULY

The word 'saunter' comes from a practice in the Middle Ages, when people would go around begging for money to help them to go to the Holy Land, or Sainte Terre. The people who did this became known as Sainte-Terreurs (saunterers).

These saunterers remind me of people I used to meet whose way of life – for whatever family or personal reason – consisted in walking and wandering, sauntering, from one part of the country to another, sleeping here and there on farms or with friends or in hostels. They hadn't much, but one thing they had was plenty of time for reflection and philosophising, and they were almost always interesting and challenging people to meet and talk to.

'Sauntering' seems to me to have still the desire for pilgrimage about it – the desire to walk a sacred path, taking time to look and listen and reflect.

What I want is to leap out of this personality
and then sit apart from that leaping –
I've lived too long where I can be reached.

RUMI

6 JULY

St Hildegard of Bingen, visionary, prophet, healer, social reformer, scientist, dramatist and composer of wonderful sacred music for women's voices, lived in a male-dominated age – the twelfth century. She called herself, in the idiom of her day, 'a poor little female'. But she was a woman of insight and wisdom and vision – a female role model completely out of her time.

For Hildegard, God and creation were lover and beloved, and she compares this mutual love to a marriage that is abundantly fruitful. It is through God's creation that we meet God, every day.

Know from the start, that the wisdom I share with you comes not from this poor creature you see before you, but from the living light . . . God works where God wills.

ST HILDEGARD OF BINGEN

7 JULY

Hospitality is love. It is an openness to the unknown and the unfamiliar; it is being open to the stranger, to what frightens us, to what we may not like. It is being prepared to accept people who may stand on our toes or rub us up the wrong way – because of course there are differences between people, and those differences may be the source of irritation, or even of pain.

We can start enthusiastically enough, but sometimes it is hard to remain open when we come up against our own insecurities. So the spirit of hospitality needs to be cherished and cultivated and fostered.

It will be worth it because hospitality, as well as being challenging, is life-giving.

[Divine love] is a love that clothes us, enfolds and embraces us and . . . completely surrounds us, never to leave us.

JULIAN OF NORWICH

Week 28

A stroll in a garden on a summer's evening can change our perspective on the whole day.

8 JULY

Celebration is not the same as going to a party, or even giving a party. True celebration celebrates and honours a person, by giving thought to the form the celebration will take so that it is appropriate for the person, by planning carefully so that it will be special for them, by finding the right gift for the person. Spontaneous celebration is fun and life-giving, but planned celebration is a way of honouring our friends in the most thoughtful way we can.

This is the day the Lord has made;
let us rejoice and be glad in it.

PSALM 118:24

9 JULY

A member of the first American team to climb Mount Everest described a profound experience he had on his way down from the peak. While stopping to admire the view he turned around and saw a small blue flower in the snow. At that moment, he said, his life was changed: 'Everything opened up and flowed together and made some strange kind of sense. And I was at complete peace.'

We all need those beautiful jolts, when it all fits together, our energy is recharged and our wonder is restored. And the way to ensure we have these moments is to be ever in a state of grateful awareness.

The most beautiful thing we can experience is the mystery.

ALBERT EINSTEIN

10 JULY

When we pray, our emptiness becomes a gift rather than a disappointment, as God fills us with love. The more needy we are, the more we know our need for God. And in humility we begin to recognise the gifts and graces bestowed on us over our lifetime.

For all these mysteries, I thank you,
for the wonder of myself, for the wonder of your works.

PSALM 139:13–14

11 JULY

Grace is pure gift, and because of this our most meaningful encounters with it will probably come at unintended times, when we are caught off guard, when our manipulative systems are at rest or otherwise occupied.

The facts of grace are simple: grace always exists, it is always available, it is always good, it is always victorious. But although grace is always there, it doesn't simply happen. It is a gift we must prepare ourselves to receive, by living life in accord with the facts of grace, even when we do not sense them directly.

Every single creature is full of God and is a book about God.

MEISTER ECKHART

12 July

There are no lengths to which we will not go to save and protect our bodies. If we cared for the world in the same way, what a different world it would be.

I will use my arm to protect my eye because they are all one body and need each other. The cosmos is the same – one web, one body. The web of the world, the body of creation, depends on all its different parts, and that is why we all carry a responsibility for the whole cosmos, to ensure that no part of it is in danger and to live our lives protecting and loving it.

He who loves the world as his body may be entrusted with the empires.

LAO TZU

13 JULY

I visited Zambia recently, and was struck by the emphasis placed on greetings there. The morning greeting is a vitally important part of the day. There are no circumstances under which a person would start work without first greeting everyone, smiling at them, enquiring how they were feeling, and blessing them, wishing them well for the day. This happens everywhere.

Greeting our friends and colleagues with a smile and a good wish brings joy to the morning.

What sunshine is to flowers, smiles are to humanity.

JOSEPH ADDISON

14 July

In celebrating each other we carry each other –
by being present to each other, by encouraging each
other and accepting each other, by willingly partici-
pating in each other's lives and burdens, by placing
ourselves in each other's place and living each other's
experience, by taking pride in each other's fruitfulness and taking joy in each other's joy. In celebrating
each other we are like a mother carrying her child.

There is only one word that can serve as a
practical rule for our whole life – reciprocity.

CONFUCIUS

Week 29

*The unexpected flare of colour in summer
bog-land is pure gift.*

15 JULY

Our ability to be surprised is the measure of our
aliveness. If we are numb, if we take things for
granted, then we are dead; but to those who are
awake to life's surprises, death lies behind, not ahead.
To live life open to surprise, in spite of all that's
dying around us, makes us even more alive.

Every bite is a surprise.

A BLIND MAN

16 JULY

Surprise is the starting point for gratitude. It opens our inner eye, because the amazing fact is that every-thing is a gift. Nothing can be taken for granted. If something can't be taken for granted, then we must be grateful. And as we begin to be grateful for small things, that gratitude grows and grows and expands and expands, like ripples on the surface of a pool. What starts it off may be a little stone, a little surprise, a little openness, but as the ripple extends it becomes more and more alive to what is given, more and more alive to the giver, and more and more alive to giving.

Expect nothing; live frugally on surprise.

ALICE WALKER

17 JULY

Every day we are bombarded with requests to become involved in things. The danger is that we will try to take them all on, but end up only being able to do them superficially.

If we want to be enriched by what we commit ourselves to, then we need to choose our commitments carefully. The unique talent given to each of us shines forth if it has time and space to be developed and fostered and attended to, which is why we need to take time for ourselves so that we can discern which situations we need to become part of.

What is this life if, full of care,
we have no time to stand and stare.

W H DAVIES

18 July

The greatest gift we can bestow is thanksgiving.
When we give thanks, we give something greater
than the gift we have received, whatever it is. In
giving gifts, we often give what we can spare, but in
giving thanks we give ourselves.

The receiver of a gift depends on the giver, but
the circle is incomplete until the giver becomes the
receiver – the receiver of thanks.

Gratitude is the awareness that life, in all it manifestations, is a gift for which we want to give
thanks.

HENRI NOUWEN

19 JULY

A sense of aliveness enters into us when we are least in control, fully open and not on our guard. These moments may be rare, but if we want to cultivate them, we need to learn to lessen our need for control.

I am a feather on the breath of God.

ST HILDEGARD OF BINGEN

20 JULY

When I pray with the people I live among – many of whom have experienced homelessness, poverty, depression and exclusion – what strikes me more than anything else is the way they are able to name and claim the moments of grace and gratitude in their lives.

They are not calculating or doing cost/benefit analyses of their lives; they simply acknowledge and recognise and are grateful for everything they have.

You pray in your distress and in your need. Would that you might pray also in the fullness of your joy and in your days of abundance.

KABRIL GIBRAN

21 JULY

Compassion is not an end in itself but part of our journey to unity. Listening more, judging less, we loosen our identification with certain models of self and begin to recognise the essence of each person we meet.

Compassion gradually becomes an offering, first to those we are with, but also to God. Helping becomes an act of reverence, worship and gratitude.

Life is a sort of splendid torch which I have got hold of for the moment and I want to make it burn as brightly as possible before handing it over to future generations.

GEORGE BERNARD SHAW

Week 30

Our hearts respond to the expanse and intensity of a fuchsia hedge, the exuberance of wild flowers.

22 JULY

Even our sufferings and losses can be occasions of grace if we recognise through them the sufferings and losses of others. Also, when we realise we are not abandoned, even if we abandon ourselves, then we are filled with grace.

Apprehend God in all things.

MEISTER ECKHART

23 JULY

We live in a world in which there is scarcity in the midst of plenty. The scarcity is real and the plenty is real, but we can also invent scarcity by keeping our gifts to ourselves and not sharing them.

Our gifts are not our own individual possessions but are given to us to share with others. And as we give, we are blessed. There is an automatic outpouring of love with giving, and, equally automatically, love comes back to us.

You should live so that it is possible to create the kingdom of love on earth.

LEO TOLSTOY

24 JULY

Just as negative behaviour is powerful, so also is positive behaviour. If we choose to love life and to love people, we will find that our positive approach will evoke positive responses. Smiles invite smiles; respect generates respect; gratitude evokes gratitude; serenity and a peaceful attitude lessen stress and tension.

O world invisible we view thee
O world intangible we touch thee
O world unknowable we know thee.

FRANCIS THOMPSON

25 July

Compassion is about living with an open heart, and the work of compassion – the work done by people who care for the sick, or work with people who are depressed or lonely or poor or excluded – is work of great spiritual value.

Seeing the work of compassion as a spiritual undertaking is in no way to diminish the importance for this work of things like training, experience, professionalism, special gifts or skills, a sense of humour. Quite the reverse – our particular talents and qualifications are more likely to come to the fore when we have a richer and more spacious sense of who we are.

He who neglects to drink
Of the spring of experience
Is apt to die of thirst
In the desert of ignorance.

LI PO

26 JULY

My introduction to the work of H D Thoreau was a worn and well-thumbed little book I received as a present from a gentle, thoughtful and self-educated old man from the west of Ireland that I met on my first trip to Boston in 1965. Frank believed in what he called 'freedom of the spirit'. He said that if people could hold on to their beliefs, their spirit would remain free and they would be able to live happy and contented lives anywhere – even in a convent!

'Read this and reread it often and it will keep you sane and free,' he told me, and that is some of the best advice I have ever been given.

Our own life is the instrument with which we experiment with truth.

THICH NHAT HANH

27 JULY

When a woman I know was diagnosed with cancer, she was devastated at first, and so was all her family, but soon she bounced back with extraordinary vitality. Once she realised that she had only a short time to live, she decided that she was going to live that time as fully as she could. She said she realised that she had lost her sense of surprise, but now she was going to rediscover it and love the surprises every day brings.

During her last three years Susan was joy to be with. She saw surprises everywhere, and she was full to overflowing with joy.

The world breaks everyone and afterward many are strong at the broken places.

ERNEST HEMINGWAY

28 JULY

Giving with compassion is not easy. It is not easy to know the pain and to feel the hurt of another. Sometimes compassion asks us simply to be with someone, to wait patiently, to experience their powerlessness with them; at other times compassion asks us to do things, to go that extra mile. Sometimes compassion asks us to receive graciously from another who is in need of our receptivity and our vulnerability.

One has not lived in vain
who learns to be unruffled by loss, by gain,
by joy, by pain.

ANGELUS SILESIUS

Week 31

As the dry earth yearns for water, the unappeasable spirit within us yearns for its source of life.

29 JULY

A woman came to me once to offer her services to people who needed looking after, but she said that the one thing she could not do would be to work with people who are dying. 'I am too soft,' she said. 'It would kill me.' I discovered, though, that it was her own death and not other people's death that really scared her. In time she came to terms with her fears, and she is now very active in a hospice for people who are dying.

This incident helped me to realise that to be of service to others, we must first face our own doubts and needs.

The body is the first student of the soul.

HENRY DAVID THOREAU

30 JULY

At times, helping happens simply in the way of things. It's not something we really think about, merely the instinctive response of an open heart. Caring is a reflex. Someone slips, your arm goes out. A car is in a ditch, you join the others and push. It all seems natural and appropriate. This is because an instinctive generosity of spirit is working in us. Not always, of course, but when it is there and we respond to it, we feel great.

Real goodness is always simple. Simplicity is so attractive and so profitable that it is strange that so few people are really simple.

LEO TOLSTOY

31 July

Wouldn't it be wonderful to have a society where the care of others didn't have to be obligatory but would occur naturally. Where service wasn't a duty but a way of living – the way of natural love and compassion. Such a society is possible. All we have to do is wish for it – and mean it.

God pours the love and the life into us, we need only be available, like the flute in order for the song of love to come to life.

RABINDRANATH TAGORE

1 August

I usually go to visit the hospice on Sundays, and the older people that I meet there give me strength and courage, and I come away feeling that the people I have visited have blessed me. When I go there I am always conscious that I am going to be blessed, even though words of blessing are never used. I think this is because old people's hands are often empty, and so they are open and ready to bless.

When I leave, I feel a renewed stamina and a deepened hope. I believe in what I am doing and that what I am about to do will be fruitful. That is what I mean when I say that I feel blessed.

To bless is to put a bit of yourself into something. It is to make holy, to change something or someone because of your presence.

MACRINA WIEDERKEHR

2 AUGUST

I noticed that a person who worked with me used to finish all her phone conversations with the expression 'God bless!' instead of goodbye. I asked her why she used that expression, and she thought for a moment and then answered that she did it because I did it, that she had picked up the habit from me.

I explained to her that I say it deliberately, that it is part of the tradition I grew up with, and that when I say it, I really do believe I am blessing the person. She was taken aback to hear that. Still, I notice that she continues to say it!

For in him we live, and move and have our being.

ACTS 17:28

3 AUGUST

Work is always community work, whether we realise it or not. Robert Frost tells a story about a farm worker who goes out to turn the hay early in the morning. The mower had cut the grass much earlier in the morning and had left, so this man turning the hay feels lonely. But then a butterfly calls his attention to the flowers that the mower had left standing because they were too beautiful to cut down. The shared experience of the flowers' beauty moves him to change his mind, and teaches him how all work intertwines.

And dreaming, as it were, held brotherly speech
With one whose thought I had not hoped to reach.

'Men work together,' I told him from the heart,
'whether they work together or apart.'

ROBERT FROST

4 AUGUST

We all experience occasional moments of deep joy, when we feel illuminated and contented, and we wish they could last for ever.

These moments do not arrive out of nowhere. It is out of our ordinary actions, choices, decisions, reflections, silences, plans, prayers and thoughts that these wonderful moments emerge: we create them for ourselves.

There lives the dearest freshness deep down things.

GERALD MANLEY HOPKINS

Week 32

The earth renews itself with quiet constancy so that it does not become a barren desert.

5 AUGUST

There is a poem by Rilke where he speaks about the rush of life, the 'hurrying life'. He warns us to look much deeper than that, to look at 'what stands behind us'.

If we do not take the time to reflect on who we are, we will succumb to the mad pace of life and become just a doing, rushing person.

I have come into this world to make
this a good place to live in,
But to live in,
be it good or bad.

HENRY DAVID THOREAU

6 August

We all need at times to discover again what is beautiful about ourselves. We stultify our beauty by trying to model ourselves on the images that are set for us by others – the way we think we should look, the way we should feel, the way we should dress, walk and talk.

If we are to nurture our own particular beauty, we must nourish our bodies with healthy food and drink; nourish our minds with literature, art and good company; nourish our spirits with silence, stillness and prayer. This way we can rid ourselves of anxiety, anger and negativity, and replace them with peace and joy and positive energy.

He who would be free must not conform.

OSCAR WILDE

7 AUGUST

For Plato, philosophy was a loving dedication to wisdom – and surprise and the ability to be surprised the beginning of philosophy.

It is because of its capacity for surprise that wisdom surpasses mere cleverness or academic achievement. Cleverness will not be surprised by the unexpected, but it is wisdom to be surprised by the expected.

. . . the eyes of my eyes are opened.

E E CUMMINGS

8 AUGUST

In receiving gifts from our creator, we become co-creators, because a gift cannot be developed unless we co-operate with it and with the giver, the creator. It is in that act of co-operation that we become co-creators, instruments in bringing the gift to fruition, so that we can in turn bestow it on others.

It is an awesome responsibility to take seriously the gifts and talents we have received and to use them to their fullest potential – to nurture them with care, love and devotion and with imagination, creativity, zeal and hard work . . . to rejoice in them and to give thanks for them, knowing they are not just for ourselves but for the good of all creation.

The gift turned inward, unable to be given becomes a heavy burden, even sometimes a kind of poison. It is as though the flow of life was backed up.

MAY SARTON

9 AUGUST

Once, when I was establishing a self-help project for older people to enable them to take control of their lives, a young man came to visit me. He was most anxious to be involved with older people because he had been very close to his grandmother, who had died suddenly the previous month. Ideas flowed out of him, some of them realistic, some not. His passion moved me so that I felt I really had to engage with him and enable him to become involved, even if some of his ideas would not work out.

Sometimes we are afraid of passion like this because we are afraid of where it will lead us. But passion can teach us to trust our instinct, and it can take us to very interesting places.

We have our brush and colours – paint
Paradise and in we go.

NIKOS KAZANTZAKIS

10 August

A few years ago I went to London to lead a one-day seminar, and I went straight from the airport to the theatre the night before the seminar. When I arrived at the theatre, I realised I had left my overnight bag in the taxi. But what could I do? I went ahead into the auditorium and hoped for the best.

At the interval I heard my name being called through a muffled loudspeaker, and when I went out to reception I found that the taxi driver had dropped off my bag. He'd got my name from my passport, and returned to the theatre. He left no name, no message, just the bag.

His kindness changed my whole trip. If ever I begin to doubt the goodness of others I think of that nameless London taxi driver.

> That best portion of a good man's life,
> His little, nameless, unremembered acts
> Of kindness and love.

WILLIAM WORDSWORTH

11 AUGUST

A wet day in summer can upset us if it interferes with our plans. So much of our life is about being in control that we become very uneasy when we feel out of control. Nature, however, seeks to establish balance and harmony, rather than power and control. Nature does not seek glory and power; it is not following an agenda; it has no vendetta. It is simply being itself. When we honour nature we learn wisdom, and it is wisdom that allows us to approach every rainy day of our lives knowing that it has meaning and holds within it new possibilities for us.

The gentle rain which waters my beans, and keeps me in the house today is not dreary and melancholy, but good for me too. Though it perverts my hoeing them, it is of far more worth than my hoeing. If it should continue so long as to cause the seeds to rot in the ground and destroy the potatoes in the lowland, it will still be good for the grass on the uplands and being good for the grass it will be good for me.

HENRY DAVID THOREAU

Week 33

*To grow spiritually is to become integrated
and fulfilled as a person. It is to become like
a tree rather than a pile of branches.*

12 AUGUST

A teacher described her vision of heaven and hell to her students. Hell, she said, was a room with a round table at which six people were seated. Each had a bowl of food and a spoon, but because the spoons they held were longer than their arms all were slowly starving. They couldn't feed themselves.

Heaven, the teacher said, was the same situation, but the people were smiling, joyful and full of health because they were using the long spoons to feed each other.

There is a courtesy of the heart
It is akin to love
Out of it rises the
Purest in our outward
Behaviour.

JOHANN WOLFGANG VON GOETHE

13 AUGUST

Christine Noble grew up in desperate poverty, experiencing humiliation, rejection, neglect and abuse both within her family and in her neighbourhood. Yet she grew into a woman of extraordinary vision, courage and strength, and she works indefatigably for the street children of Vietnam.

In spite of her own horrific childhood, Christine goes on and on, doing more and more for children caught up in all kinds of dangerous and dreadful situations. Where does she get her enthusiasm from? I think it is because she believes that anything that any one of us can do to help any person to feel more lovable is the most important thing on this earth.

You are only one person, they said, But when I was a child, I needed only one person to love me. One is very important.

CHRISTINE NOBLE

14 AUGUST

We all know the parable Jesus told about the vine-
yard owner who hired workers at various times
during the day and yet paid them all the same
amount. Those who had worked hard in the vine-
yard all day were annoyed that they had been paid
the same as the workers who came at the end of the
day and had worked only for a short while. But the
employer said that he had made a bargain with all
of them, and the fact that he had made a more
generous bargain with those who came last was no
reason for those who came early to be envious. The
moral of the parable is that the first shall be last and
the last shall be first.

Our sympathies are naturally with the workers
who toiled all day but received no more than the
ones who came at the eleventh hour. But that is our
logic. This parable is about God's logic.

I have summoned you by name; you are mine.

ISAIAH 43:1

15 AUGUST

On Saturday afternoon, 15 August 1998, thirty people were murdered by a terrorist bomb in the town of Omagh in County Tyrone in Northern Ireland. Exactly one week later, to the very hour and minute, the people of Ireland were invited to stand in silence to remember Omagh, and we did. Hundreds and thousands of men, women and children stopped and remembered the people who had been killed, injured and bereaved.

I stood at that moment in a little church on Achill Island and it struck me, as we stood together in solidarity and mourning, that the bombing of Omagh was not just the evil act of a small group, but was also connected to our evil, my evil and yours – our lack of peace with ourselves and with others, our refusal to forgive. If our act of solidarity meant anything, it had to be a turning outward with a new promise of bringing about peace and justice.

Time changes nothing, people do.

ANCIENT PROVERB

16 AUGUST

Once when I was very sad, a friend of mine, a psychologist, sent me a book of cartoons – not a word or a line, just a book of cartoons. Well, I laughed and laughed; they were all so ridiculous, as is so much of life. It helped me enormously.

Mark Twain once said that people who overstay their welcome couldn't just be thrown out the window but must be coaxed a step at a time towards the door. This is how we have to deal with our pain too, just a step at a time towards the door.

People show their character in nothing more clearly than in what they think laughable.

JOHANN WOLFGANG VON GOETHE

17 AUGUST

Creativity is a power of expression, and when that method of expression is denied people, the power has to be expressed in another way. When people are forced to leave their homes and homeland and the sources of their creativity, for example, it is not surprising if they succumb to violence to give expression to their power.

When the creative spirit within us is released and given expression, our lives are relaxed, convivial and more joy-filled. Creativity may be the richest source of answers to overcrowded prisons, to unemployment and under-employment, to the problems of children who leave school early and to destructive and oppressive regimes.

Creativity is a spiritual action in which a person forgets about himself, moves outside of himself, absorbed by his task.

NIKOLAI BERDYAEV

18 AUGUST

Where we have poverty, unemployment, displacement, dispossession and powerlessness, the lights have gone out and what we are left with are drugs, crime, violence and alcoholism – symptoms of darkness. In nations that spend hundreds of billions on warfare and weaponry and a pittance on eradicating poverty and misery, the lights have gone out. And where billions are spent by the rich on superfluities when millions live in want, the lights have gone out.

We cannot change all these things but we can bring our creative powers to bear on these situations. We can look at things afresh. And when we do this, we find sources within ourselves that will make a difference.

Our light may not be dynamic, but even a flickering wick of creativity could make all the difference.

Without creativity the lights will go out.

CARL R ROGERS

Week 34

*Bees orient themselves by sunshine even when
the sun is hidden behind the clouds.*

19 AUGUST

One morning as I walked to early mass, the sky was
beginning to turn blue. When I left the church half
an hour later, the sky was totally transformed. It
looked as if it had been painted in magnificent shades
of pink and red, intermingled with blue and green.

That morning I saw what I had hardly ever seen
before – shapes of the spaces in the sky. I felt as if
I was seeing the world entirely anew. Everything –
every tree, every leaf – seemed to be speaking to me.
The air, the light, the objects, even my own body
seemed porous and exposed. A window to another
dimension of life was opened to me.

That experience lasted the whole morning and
then the window closed. I cannot explain this experience in any scientific way, but it was a glimpse of
the divine energy of God.

If we lack beauty in our lives
We will probably suffer similar
disturbances in the soul.

THOMAS MORE

20 AUGUST

Our freedom as human beings is grounded in forgiveness. Forgiveness liberates us from the roles we get ourselves cemented into, the sense we have of being oppressed, wounded, offended. The truth is that we are all in turn offended and offender, oppressed and oppressor, wounded and wounder, and through forgiveness we recognise that complexity.

Forgiving others requires that we re-open the path that disappointment has closed and that failure has barricaded. The experience of forgiveness leads to a sense of celebration that enables us to understand our own wretchedness and to accept our failures. We are released to go in peace to resume our roles as responsible members of the community.

A man that studieth revenge keeps his own wounds green.

FRANCIS BACON

21 AUGUST

Today more than ever, in our busy, stressful world we need to take the time and the space to care for ourselves. It is only from having a right relationship with ourselves that we can form right relationships with others, with society, with the universe. And through forming right relationships with our Creator and with God and with the rest of creation, we come back again to a new sense of ourselves and of our own beauty and preciousness.

For everything flowers from within, of self-blessing.

GALWAY KINNEL

22 AUGUST

We ourselves are the universe, we ourselves are creation. The land we stand on, the created land, is holy ground, and we are connected to it and part of it.

All we need in order to realise this is intense awareness. If we can awaken our awareness of the connectedness of all things then we will also become aware of our connectedness with the creator of all things.

Madame Butterfly was dictated to me by God; I was merely instrumental in putting it on paper and communicating it to the public.

GIACOMO PUCCINI

23 AUGUST

It is one thing to forgive others but quite another to receive forgiveness. Openness to forgiveness from others demands that we meet the next moment with new perception and an open heart, that we leave behind us the dust of former quarrels and bickerings and unpleasant encounters.

Forgiveness is the answer to the dream of a child, a miracle in which an object, broken in pieces, is still intact, and a soiled one is still clean. This, however, cannot happen if something is left unresolved between us and our neighbour.

DAG HAMMARSKJÖLD

24 AUGUST

Sometimes we can be so busy we lose sight of what is important for the sake of the urgent and the immediate.

When a monk at the abbey of Clairvaux was elected Pope Eugene III, his former abbot, St Bernard, wrote him a lengthy letter of love and concern. The first time I read it, I felt it was a personal letter to me. I felt I needed a Bernard in my life to slow me down, to stop me in my tracks.

It is far wiser for you to withdraw from time to time from your affairs, than let your affairs draw you and drive you, step by step, to where you certainly do not want to go. You ask where? To the point where the heart is hardened. Do not ask any further what this means – if you are not alarmed now, your heart is already there.

ST BERNARD OF CLAIRVAUX

25 August

It is easy to slip into the habit of fulfilling people's expectations of us. If people expect us to work hard for very long hours, for example, with little time off and for little compensation, they see us as people who are generous with our time and ourselves. And so, even when we feel tired, exhausted and used, we go on living up to others' expectations, but we feel angry and resentful underneath.

The reason for this is that we are afraid that if we changed the situation, we might then be perceived as failures. And if we failed, we would have to own our own failure. But we have a right and a duty to own and to name and to control who we are, what we do and how we do it. Only then can we live according to our own lights, at our own pace and in our own size.

For I tell you the truth, many prophets and righteous men longed to see what you see but did not see it and to hear what you hear but did not hear it.

MATTHEW 13:17

Week 35

*The earth has a voice of its own and by
listening to it birds find their way home
from distant places.*

26 AUGUST

Nurturing a grudge can become a full-time pre-
occupation. Unspoken anger does not bring us
freedom, but instead keeps us locked to the other
person. The glue of unresolved resentment keeps us
stuck in silent pain.

Are there really people in our lives who have done
things so bad that they deserve to be ignored? Yet
that is often the weapon we employ when we are
hurt or angry. If instead we can learn to be assertive,
to express our hurt and anger, we can release
emotional joy and freedom and through this find the
ability to be honest, clear and direct. That is the
beginning of forgiveness.

Nothing hurts worse than being ignored.

ANON

27 AUGUST

I'm always a bit perplexed when people ask me how I keep going; how I keep doing what I'm doing, working with people on the margins of society; how I come up with new ideas. This to me is like asking parents how they live with their children. When we really love people we recognise their inherent worth and dignity and working with them grows out of the process of loving.

Unfortunately we live in a society that teaches us to distrust the fundamental goodness and wisdom of our nature, but I believe that when we enter into the wisdom within us, we enter into the mystery of divine love. And it is that central core of love in the universe that keeps us going.

But the artist persists because he has the will to create, and this is the magic power which can transform and transfigure and transpose and which will ultimately be transmitted to others.

ANAÏS NIN

28 AUGUST

Not long ago I was standing in a queue alongside a young woman with a four-year-old boy. The child was entertaining himself by rolling around on the floor looking at everyone and everything from every possible angle. His mother's only concern was to get him to stand up. She apologised to the rest of us for his behaviour.

As I watched him, I was struck by the contrast between his behaviour and the behaviour of the rest of us – sedate, composed, orderly, minding our own business. The child's behaviour was not offensive, but my sympathy was with his mother, and it struck me that we all need order in our lives. We need to have room for creative, aimless play, but we also need people to help us to have order – as this child needed his mother.

Beauty from order springs.

WILLIAM KING

29 AUGUST

People of goodness do not need to bestow blessings;
instead, they become a blessing. Their presence is
goodness and they engender new life, strength,
healing, courage and vitality by their presence. That
was exactly how Jesus blessed the people around
him.

Just to live is a blessing
Just to live is holy.

RABBI ABRAHAM HESCHEL

30 AUGUST

Few of us can manage as adults to recapture the sheer delight of the creative, meaningless play of the child. But we can grow at any age in our ability to be playful.

Playfulness does not have to prove anything; it is not competitive; it has no why; it has no goal. Pure play – not the sort of play that has rules, like playing tennis or football, but pure, childish play – is spontaneous celebration.

The most important thing is to create; nothing else matters, creation is all.

PABLO PICASSO

31 AUGUST

As we are blessed at our birth in the act of creation, so we in our turn are commanded to bless. To bless is to say good things, to radiate goodness.

All creation is sacred. If we are aware of the inherent sacredness and beauty of all creation we will bless all and be blessed by all and we will communicate the life and beauty of God in and all around us, calling forth what is best in all of us.

The command to bless is engraved in all our hearts. Whether we understand it or not matters little. Whether we agree or disagree makes no difference. In our hearts we know it: we are blessed and are called to bless, to say good things, to radiate goodness from the core of our being.

May you be blessed Lord God of our ancestor, be praised and extolled forever.

DANIEL 3:52

September/October

As we gather in the harvest *of the garden's fruitfulness we are in* harmony *with the universe.*

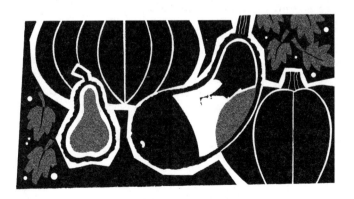

For eight months we have toiled and enjoyed our garden. We've grown to love its barrenness, its emptiness, its silences. We have sown the seeds of joy, beauty, love and authenticity with hope and courage. We have watched them growing and enjoyed their blossoming. Now we enjoy the gathering in, the fruitfulness of the garden, and we see the harmony and interconnectedness of the whole garden of our life, which is part of the garden of the universe, the Creator's garden.

1 SEPTEMBER

There was a time when I prayed each morning to ask God to assist me in my daily work. Now I ask God to allow me to assist him in his creative work today.

That makes all the difference, because it acknowledges that the best we can do in our short time on earth is co-operate with God and his work, knowing that God wills only what is best for all of us and that it is our privilege to assist in his creation.

Be so true to thyself as thou be not false to others.

FRANCIS BACON

Week 36

*Hospitality is to the heart what
fruitfulness is to the garden.*

2 SEPTEMBER

On a recent visit to Solweisi in Zambia, I woke up
one morning to hear that a snake had been killed
during the night. It had entered the vicinity where I
was staying, and had devoured a little dog. A
watchman saw the snake and struck it. After
vomiting the dog, who was by then dead, the snake
also died.

This was a particularly dangerous type of snake,
that could devour a person, but it was also very
beautiful, and it was sad to see it lying there. I
suddenly became aware of the underlying unity of
all life as I stood there looking at the snake. I realised
that all things in life – beautiful and reprehensible,
dangerous and benign – take sustenance from the
earth.

All are but parts of one stupendous whole,
whose body Nature is, and God the soul.

ALEXANDER POPE

3 SEPTEMBER

The dreadful danger in which our planet exists is directly caused by our unthinking collusion with attitudes and systems that poison earth daily and hourly, rather than revering her as mother and sister – attitudes such as the desire to dominate and to acquire, and systems such as unthinking militarism and unnecessary consumption.

Prayer to the Grass
Let me so walk upon you and even though you must bend your head under me as I pass by, you will know after I am gone that I am your sister.

NATIVE AMERICAN PRAYER

4 SEPTEMBER

The great Rhineland visionary, St Hildegard of Bingen, saw divine presence in the environment. She coined the term *veriditas* to express nature's power to nurture life. Her writings were filled with metaphors of verdancy – 'the verdancy of justice', 'the greening power of faith', 'the vigour that hugs the world'.

Hildegard's spirituality was a tapestry of faith, compassion and love of the earth. She measured the health and well-being of people and situations according to their harmony with nature.

The air
With its penetrating strength
Characterises
The victorious banner that is trust.
It gives night
To the fire's flame
And sprinkles
The imagination of believers
With the dew of hope.

ST HILDEGARD OF BINGEN

5 SEPTEMBER

Sometimes when we feel relaxed, we feel like humming, singing or dancing. At times we can even sense that we are not just singing a song, we are not just listening to music – we are the music, we are the song. We are not just doing steps in rhythm, we are the dance. This happens when we lose the distance and separateness that are part of our everyday lives and instead feel a connectedness to that deep undercurrent that forms the rhythm of the universe itself. It is the same rhythm that makes day follow night and spring follow winter.

The birds I heard today which fortunately did not come within the scope of my science, sang especially as if it had been the first morning of creation.

HENRY DAVID THOREAU

6 SEPTEMBER

Before we can truly experience our connectedness with the earth and the animals and all creation, we need to be connected within ourselves. We need to learn how to be contented and at home in our own company, to know how to take time alone. The more we know ourselves, the more we see our connection with others.

We can only love others when we love ourselves, and we can only learn to love our community and the community of all people when we recognise that everything and everyone is related to everything and everyone else because the divine is in each and every one of us.

The beauty of the world hath made me sad,
This beauty that will pass.

PATRICK PEARSE

7 SEPTEMBER

One act of peace can effect peace throughout the world, just as one act of violence touches us all, because we are what our actions are. While we are making peace, we are becoming and being peace.

The truly wise person kneels at the feet of all creatures.

MECHTILD OF MAGDEBURG

8 SEPTEMBER

Awareness that we are a unique part of the unity that is the universe leads us to a greater compassion for ourselves and for all beings. It enables us to see the beauty of all creation and to become more willing and eager to reach out to one another with openness.

Each time we are able to reach out from inside our heart to someone else's pain, despite our fear and defensiveness, we nurture a love that becomes increasingly unconditional and the barriers between us and others dissolve.

If you were a poet you would see clearly that there is a cloud floating in this sheet of paper. Without a cloud there would be no rain, without rain the trees cannot grow and without trees we cannot make paper. The cloud is essential for the paper to exist.

THICH NHAT HANH

Week 37

If we give a plant space it flourishes: if we celebrate each person's uniqueness nobody will feel excluded.

9 SEPTEMBER

We have more room in our hearts for some people than for others. For some people we have no room at all. We can remain like that or we can allow the idea of hospitality to challenge us, and to lead us to new possibilities, new friends.

New ideas and new possibilities are imprisoned inside our hearts, inside ourselves and inside our homes. Things change because what we take in opens us and changes us.

If there is room in the heart there is room in the house.

DANISH PROVERB

10 SEPTEMBER

In the traditional community in which I grew up, people 'lived in each other's shadow' (as the story-teller Peig Sayers put it). They visited each other, sat around the fire in the evenings and told stories and worked co-operatively to get the harvest in or the crops sown.

These people had little money, but they weren't as poor as some country communities were. They had plenty to eat and had access to fuel. They had their own non-monetary economy, and they could rely on each other in times of need. In fact they had everything but money – which is to have much.

Praise him, sun and moon,
    praise him, all you shining stars.
Praise him, you highest heavens
    and your waters above the skies.
Praise the Lord from the earth,
    you great sea creatures and all ocean depths,
lightning and hail, snow and clouds,
stormy winds that do his bidding.

PSALM 148:3–4, 7–8

11 SEPTEMBER

We live in a society that tells us that in order to be successful we must work hard – forty, fifty, even up to sixty hours a week. This drive for success makes people unhealthy and dispirited, but it is easy to be seduced into such a self-destructive way of life, because of the promise of success and reward that it holds out.

This way of life thrives on fear – fear of failure, fear of losing our individuality, fear of giving up something of ourselves, fear of not being in control. Most especially it thrives on fear of love itself, the fear of being opened by the force and call of love, the fear of entering into reciprocity.

Never try to justify your deeds to other people.

LEO TOLSTOY

12 SEPTEMBER

In the Ireland in which I grew up, the simple acts of everyday life – rising and going to rest, the lighting of candles, the keeping in of the embers overnight and the rekindling of the fire in the morning, the sowing, the reaping, the harvesting, buying and selling, life and death – all had a place in the rhythm of a way of life that was truly incantational.

If we think of life as a circle continuously flowing, we will see our whole life as unity, and in this integrated and harmonious life, a simple act such as opening the curtains or the window, letting in God's light and air, is a prayer, if we allow it to uplift our minds to God.

Those who raise their thoughts to heaven will always have clear days because the sun always shines above the clouds.

LEO TOLSTOY

13 SEPTEMBER

A man I met recently who told me he gave £5,000 a year to be divided between charities and political parties. That was his contribution to healing the ills of society. This man was well known for not caring about the welfare of his staff and for employing young people as cheap labour, so I asked him if he saw any connection between the way he ran his business and the rest of society. He said no – he worked hard, he gave employment, and felt that in setting aside money for the less fortunate he was carrying out his responsibility. It struck me that this is how most of us live our lives: we do our best with our work and we leave the rest to somebody else.

It is easy enough to give to charity, but it is much more difficult to take responsibility for injustices we know about. It is much easier to do general good than to do good in minute particulars.

He who would do good to another must do it in Minute Particulars. General Good is the plea of the Scoundrel, hypocrite and flatterer.

WILLIAM BLAKE

14 SEPTEMBER

Most of our lives are lived indoors, often with locked doors and windows that do not open, walled-in in homes, offices or cars. Living inside makes it all too easy to live inside our heads, inside our own little comfort zones.

Walking around the streets connects us with the real world, especially if we walk around at different times and in different parts of the town or city. This helps us to open not only our eyes and ears but also our hearts as citizens of the world.

The frog does not drink up the pond in which he lives.

INDIAN PROVERB

15 SEPTEMBER

I remember an old man telling me how his father at the age of eighty walked ten miles every day for two months to visit his ailing wife in hospital. I know a mother who went without sleep for six months to care for her young baby with spina bifida.

People go to all kinds of lengths for love. When we give ourselves in love, we can break all the norms. This is the mystery of love. When one gives oneself in love there is a new delight in being alive, new powers of awareness and perception. In love we enlarge our boundaries and accept our limitations. We forgive ourselves and learn a new way of living.

The only gift is a portion of thyself.

RALPH WALDO EMERSON

Week 38

Fear is a weed that can strangle us if we let it.

16 SEPTEMBER

In sacred scripture, the word success never appears – instead, we have the word fruitful and the phrases 'bearing much fruit', 'bearing fruit in due season'.

There is a world of difference between being successful and being fruitful. If we seek only to be successful, then we are concerned with outcome, results. We all like to see a task or work completed, but when we become obsessed with completions, results, success, we miss the pleasure and joy of the process, the doing of the task. If we are seeking to be fruitful, on the other hand, we are concerned with the whole process, not just the outcome, and *how* we do what we do is as important as *what* we do.

If a man remains in me and I in him he will bear much fruit.

JOHN 15:5

17 SEPTEMBER

Some say wisdom is about pure knowledge. Some say wisdom is about being adventurous. Some think wisdom is being prudent.

Wisdom is knowing who we are as human beings. It is the sum of what we've learnt through our experience, through the risks that we've taken, the people we've met, the loves we've shared, the insights we've gained.

Wisdom is the way we connect the facts we have accumulated with what we intuitively know. Wisdom is the acceptance that life is a mixture of light and darkness, of dying and rising, of joys and sorrows, of beauty and ugliness.

Wisdom is having an inner peace in the midst of agitation and struggle, in the midst of insecurity and even disorder. Wisdom is about being open to learning from everything and everyone, however pleasant or unpleasant.

Be a lantern to yourself and a refuge. Draw close to the light within yourself and seek no other shelter.

BUDDHIST WISDOM

18 September

Imagine what it would be like if the animal world was as competitive as the human world. Birds would try to destroy each other's nests. Bees would kill each other to get at the nectar, and the more honey they made the more honour they would expect to receive.

Certainly animals sometimes have to compete over territory, nests, mates and food, but their competition is about the process of living; they compete to survive – they don't survive to compete. They set no goals. They live every day without the need to win or lose.

Imagine, on the other hand, what our lives would be like without the success and failure syndrome. Success and failure could be seen as learning experiences. If we could live by sharing rather than by competing, if we didn't constantly have to measure our success by the failure of others, we could go at our own pace and choose what is right for us.

I sell mirrors in the city of the blind.

KABIR

19 SEPTEMBER

My mother used to express her thanks by saying, 'I am much obliged.' People today hardly ever say that, and I think it is because people don't like acknowledging their dependence on other people.

There is of course a healthy side to this desire to be self-sufficient, but really, self-sufficiency is an illusion, and sooner or later life will shatter that illusion. None of us would be who we are or where we are if it were not for our parents, or our teachers, or our friends. Even our enemies help to make us who we are and what we are. There are no self-made people. Every one of us needs others. Sooner or later, life brings this truth home to us. It may be a sickness, it may be a breakdown in relationships, it may be a sudden bereavement, it may be an illness, but in some way life catches us by surprise and makes us realise that we are all interdependent on each other.

There is no evil in this world. All evil exists in our souls and can be destroyed.

LEO TOLSTOY

20 SEPTEMBER

When part of ourselves – the part we are ashamed of – is hidden, it can cause us problems, for what we hide from ourselves is a sort of enemy within. However, if we look straight at that part of ourselves, if we understand it and embrace it, we can turn it into a gift. Facing up to our shadow side forces us to acknowledge that nothing is all black or white, but that everything is made up of shades of grey. We can look at the wider context, at groups, communities, neighbourhoods, nations, in the same way. On their own they are not all good or bad. They are a mixture, and no one of them is the cause of all the evil in the community or in the world. Good and evil are in all our hearts, and it is only when we acknowledge that, do we carry our responsibility for the good and evil in society.

If only there were evil people somewhere insidiously committing evil deeds and it were necessary only to separate them from the rest of us and destroy them. But the line dividing good and evil cuts through the heart of every human being.

ALEKSANDR SOLZHENITSYN

21 September

Years spent in religious study and prayer, without being involved with people who feel and are excluded and rejected, would not have given me the same sense of communion with God that I have now.

My brothers and sisters, the people I live and work among, have taught me to trust and have reverence for the world around me, to be surprised by the sacredness of the everyday, and to believe that great things are always happening and waiting to happen without our knowing it.

This sense of reverence that I have learnt from the people I work with has helped me to understand the difference between knowing *about* and really knowing.

The voice of the people has something divine.

FRANCIS BACON

22 SEPTEMBER

When I was growing up on the Dingle peninsula in County Kerry, in the 1940s and 1950s, the community had a strong sense of occasion. We celebrated marriages, baptisms, wakes, 'the stations', people emigrating and people returning. We celebrated the seasons, when the turf was footed and brought home, the harvest and the putting away of the turf for the winter.

The tradition known as 'the stations' was a carry-over from penal times when people were forbidden from practising their religion in a church. Instead, each household in turn hosted a mass: the people broke the bread of the Eucharist together, and afterwards the festivities lasted into the night.

All communities everywhere have celebrations of various types, but what I remember best about our celebrations was their inclusivity – nobody was excluded and we celebrated not so much events as each other.

Friendship is the fast root in my heart, it is like a white rose in the wilderness.

PEIG SAYERS

Week 39

Decomposition and decay alert us to the cyclic nature of life.

23 SEPTEMBER

Fear can make enemies out of people who could be friends. Fear can choke us, close us off, stifle smiles, encouragement and hope. Most of our fears are ill founded, based on poor self-esteem or a sense of inadequacy; our sense that others are better than we are.

We can give into these feelings of inadequacy and live all our lives in that greatest of fears, fear of fear itself. Or we can look at our fear and (unless it is a deep psychological fear that needs professional help) turn it on its head and replace it with a touch of reality.

When we can change the way we think, we can change everything. It is a waste of time and energy to live a life based on fear, which in turn is based on a false rating of ourselves. If we cannot change our behaviour we can at least change the way we rate ourselves and the standards we set for ourselves.

What is fear but fear of fear?

KABRIL GIBRAN

24 September

Our obsession with possessions is incredible. We collect things only to cast them aside. Things we may never need again we hold on to. Our wants can go way beyond our needs, and may become greed.

The more we give in to our wants, the more out of control our life becomes. It gets filled with clutter and chaos, confusion and crisis. Living simply, attending only to our needs, we can feel liberated and empowered. Simplicity frees us from false values and releases us from possessions so that we may free ourselves of the past and live more fully in the present.

A persistent simplification will create an inner and outer well-being that places harmony in one's life.

PEACE PILGRIM

25 SEPTEMBER

What good does love do if we are kind and good to some people and then scream at others? If we are impolite on the road, if we shove our way on the pavements, if we push our way onto an already crowded bus or train, we do not love. If we are rude to our staff, if we look with disdain on the poor, if we step over homeless people on the street, if we ignore elderly people who are struggling with their shopping, if we work only so that we look good, if we boast about our good deeds, we do not love. If we are nice and civil and polite with people we like and ignore or put down people we don't like, we do not love and we fail to see the interconnections between ourselves and others.

Drinking a cup of green tea, I stopped the war.

THOMAS MERTON

26 September

When John Donne wrote that 'no man is an island . . . any man's death diminishes me' he could have added that no part of nature is an island and that every living thing is connected to humanity as well as a part of the main. All nature is linked in a dynamic web of life. Loss in nature is also a loss for humanity, and we are all responsible for maintaining the harmony of the universe.

We are unaware of the harmony of the world most of the time, and so, perhaps out of carelessness or neglect, we interfere with it, destroying the world with our wastefulness and our greed. If we remember that we are part of a much bigger picture, and that what we do in our little place may have huge effects in other parts of the world, we may learn to respect and preserve the harmony of the universe.

Whatever befalls the earth befalls the son and daughters of the earth.

CHIEF SEATTLE

27 SEPTEMBER

The greatest gift we can give another person is our full attention. To do this we must have a certain detachment. But detachment is not hate or indifference. It is the opposite.

Indifference is not noticing the other. Detachment on the other hand is the ability to see others as being as important as we are. Detachment is the freedom to be so truly present to the other that our only concern is their comfort at that moment. When we realise that we all need one another's presence in order to move forward together, as well as individually, we cannot be indifferent.

Every organism has one and only one need in life, to fulfil its own potential.

ROLLO MAY

28 SEPTEMBER

Sometimes we have to trust that part of ourselves that is most like God, that pure spirit within us and within the whole creation, that place of remembrance which is the divine within us, the divine spirit which gathers us all into one.

Remembering, in the sense of putting the members together, can be a spiritual activity. The more we remember, the more we become complete in ourselves and part of the whole, reaching back in time, connecting with history. Remembering is embracing the whole world, embracing what is almost the unembraceable.

For a thousand years in your sight
are like a day that has just gone by,
or like a watch in the night.

PSALM 90:4

29 SEPTEMBER

We all have moments when joy returns to us in the midst of darkness and struggle. Moments of joy in our lives may seem to be forgotten, but they simply fade, dimmed by other situations or experiences. All we need is to discover ways in which we can access and remember the things of beauty and the moments of joy that lie buried within us.

I find that keeping a treasury – a book of treasured memories of people, sayings, words, experiences, events that brought joy to me at different times during my life – helps me to retrieve my memories. Returning to that treasury, especially at difficult times in my life, can bring back beauty and joy as vividly as the day I first experienced it.

Some happy tone
Of meditation, slipping in between
The beauty coming and the beauty gone.

WILLIAM WORDSWORTH

Week 40

The unstinting generosity of the autumn yield challenges our materialistic, selfish tendencies.

30 SEPTEMBER

If we let God's love be expressed through us, then all we need is to be open to it, waiting for it, empty for it. All we need do is seek it, desire it, pray for it, and the melody of God's love will flow through our different personalities and through the personal events in our lives.

If we take the time to be still and to be present to ourselves and our God each day, and do that faithfully, even for only five or ten minutes, in that time we will find ourselves in a different mind set, a mind that knows that it is not what we do that matters, but why and how we do it.

The soul is where the inner and outer world meet.

NOVALIS

1 OCTOBER

Thich Nhat Hanh, the Vietnamese Buddhist monk and peacemaker, is the great example of one whose only goal in life is to be an instrument of truth and peace. He demonstrates over and over again that each of us possesses an extraordinary and unique gift – our way of expressing divinity on earth. When we carry out our daily work with love, care and mindfulness, he says, whether it is cooking or baking or driving or writing or walking or talking, we are following the path of truth and peace and justice and bringing peace on earth in a more profound and expansive way then we can imagine.

Our own life is the instrument with which we experiment with truth.

THICH NHAT HANH

2 OCTOBER

There is nothing – no person, no thing, no thought, no experience, no sadness or joy – nothing too small or nothing too great that cannot be gathered and used for the nourishment, the beauty and the good of all. Why is it then that we have so many leftovers in life? So many opportunities missed, so many people, thoughts, ideas, things discarded, so much potential unexplored?

I believe the reason we live so dimly and miss so much is that we have never really learnt to be fully present to ourselves, to others, to experiences and events, to our creator. We have never learnt how to be present with quality. We are too busy to be present, too blinkered with our busyness to see the real beauty in the fragments and crumbs of life, and so we limp along feebly, half alive, not noticing that there should be no leftovers, unaware that nothing should be lost.

In imagining possibilities human beings act as prophets of their own existence.

PAUL RICOEUR

3 OCTOBER

Many of us were taught about God rather than encouraged to know God. We are like children who have been separated from their parents at a very young age and whose only knowledge of them has come from photo albums and stories. Our alienation from God is a deeply felt deprivation, but often it is a misunderstood deprivation – deprived people do not know what they are deprived of, because they have never known or been helped to know God, who is the Divine in them.

Nature and God I neither knew
Yet both so well knew me
They started like executors
Of my identity.

EMILY DICKINSON

4 OCTOBER

Meister Eckhart tells us that the reason we do not bear fruit is that we do not let go and let be, we do not trust ourselves or God. It is only when we trust that we can love. And if we do trust, then God can accomplish great things through us and in us.

The more we grow in trust and hope, the more we will recognise our connection with other people and with the world. To wait in hope is to come to a knowledge of connectedness.

It is only by forgetting ourselves that we draw near to God.

HENRY DAVID THOREAU

5 OCTOBER

Everywhere we look we see images of violence, in our homes, on our streets, in our schools. We see it in advertising, in films, on the news. We see it in strife within companies, communities and nations, and between them. We find it expressed physically, sexually, emotionally and psychologically. It is everywhere and we feel powerless in the face of it.

Let's just stop it. Let the writers, producers, editors and actors who portray violence stop. Let the media stop presenting stories on violence. Let parents and teachers, brothers and sisters, men and women and children stop. Let the political, social, economic, judicial and religious institutions stop.

Let us all spend time in silence, stillness, meditation and prayer each day, drawing on the spirit within us to lead us into kindness, openness of heart, goodness, well-being, generosity and goodwill.

How beautiful on the mountains are the feet of those who bring good news.

ISAIAH 52:7

6 OCTOBER

I remember a morning fifty years ago when my father
came home from cutting turf to tell us that another
turf-cutter had discovered a skeleton, which was
believed to be over a thousand years old. We were
mesmerised to learn that the bog could preserve
anything for that long. More recently I was travelling
with an artist in County Mayo when he stopped the
car, took a walk in the bog and picked up a delicate
piece of bog deal. Back in the car he told me that this
piece of wood was probably more than five thousand
years old. I felt it as a connection between our time
and times very long gone in Ireland. The bog, with its
extraordinary capacity to preserve the past, helps us
to realise that we are all part of the rhythm of life. We
are as essential to preserving the connections between
things as the bog is to holding history for us. We can
shape our destiny as the bog can shape the wood.

Everything that is in the heavens, on the earth
and under the earth, is penetrated with connectedness, penetrated with relatedness.

MEISTER ECKHART

Week 41

Harvest is a time to forget hardships of the past and rejoice in the abundance of the present.

7 OCTOBER

Recently I was guest of honour at an award ceremony in a school. The awards covered a wide range of cultural, social, spiritual, artistic and academic achievements, gifts and talents. Clearly in this school education was seen not as something purely academic but as a process of becoming full human beings. The children were taught to co-operate with one another, to appreciate each other and to rejoice in each other's promises, hopes and fruitfulness.

I could not help wondering what life would be like for these children when they left that caring school and entered the materialistic, consumer-orientated, achievement-driven world. But then I thought, if they have acquired the right values at school and at home, these values will sustain them in the future.

Do and dare what is right
Not swayed by the whim of the moment
Bravely take hold of the real
Not dallying now with what might be.

DIETRICH BONHOEFFER

8 OCTOBER

During the 1980s I was doing some work for the European Union and sending monthly reports to Brussels. They wanted to receive my reports more speedily, so bought a fax machine for my office in Dublin. The first time I used the fax machine I did so with a certain relief, glad to be able to take a rest from it for another ten days or so, when I expected a response from Brussels. Next morning, I found pages and pages strewn across the floor – my report returned with comments and questions. I decided then and there that I was not going to allow modern technology to rule me, but that I was going to use it to take pressure off rather than put pressure on. I continue to use phones, faxes and email, but I try to use them on my terms, in a way that will help me to do what I do better.

Step softly under snow or rain,
To find the place where man can pray
The way is all so very plain
That one may lose the way.

G K CHESTERTON

9 OCTOBER

Harvest is a joyful, fulfilling time, but it can also be a time of worry and risk. We have to judge the right time to gather the crop, not knowing whether we should wait another week or go for it now, not knowing whether the sun will lavish its rays and make the crop more wonderful still or whether the rain might come and destroy it. Putting off the harvest in the hope of a perfect yield is attractive, but it is a risky business.

The secret is to know when enough is enough for now. The wise harvester knows that the harvest is about reaping *all* the fruits of life, all the joys and sorrows, fears and hopes; what worked and what didn't work; those whom we loved and those whom we didn't. The wisdom of the harvester is in knowing how to reap the good and winnow the chaff with freedom and gratitude, without fear or worry.

Sow for yourself righteousness,
reap the fruit of unfailing love.

HOSEA 10:12

10 OCTOBER

In childhood we see life as a great adventure that includes everyone and everything. Part of our life's task is to reclaim the child in us. Being childlike, we realise that we matter, that our unique contribution has huge implications for the whole universe, that the part we play touches all life everywhere and for all time. We are all part of the whole, linked by our decisions and our choices to all others on the earth now and in the future, because they are all connected with us. As we walk life's journey realising that we are connected with all that has gone before and all that is present, we are preparing for the future.

The human did not weave the web of life – they are merely strands in it. Whatever they do to the web they do to themselves.

CHIEF SEATTLE

11 OCTOBER

I've always been attracted to magnanimous people, people with big minds and big hearts. Magnanimity is about authentic living, truth and justice. The magnanimous person is a passionate person who is never caught up with what is petty or small-minded.

We know the magnanimous person the moment we meet them. Their love is whole-hearted, an expression of their broad minds and generous hearts. They never get caught up in detail, in finding fault, in nit-picking, in gossip, in backbiting, for they are generous of heart, and they single out the important things that need to be tended to and give their undivided attention and energy to them. A magnanimous person challenges us to be true to ourselves and to live lives of integrity, truth and justice.

Those who have only the knowledge which can be received by our five senses do not know the essence of things. Real knowledge is the understanding that there is an inner being in everything.

INDIAN WISDOM

12 OCTOBER

Wisdom is not knowing as well as knowing, and being at peace with that uncertainty. It is about awareness and it is about wonder. It is about stopping and noticing phenomena in the world around us – air, water, wind, light, gravity, birth, rocks, heartbeats – and appreciating and understanding them.

To glean wisdom we must keep ourselves open and receptive and perceptive. Wisdom comes from boldness, from participation and tolerance, uncertainty, confusion, ignorance, suspicion, pain, suffering, joy, laughter, fun and love. Wisdom comes from our participation in and appreciation of all things in our mind, heart, body and spirit.

People may ask you, 'How do you know God?' You should respond, 'Because he is my heart.' Can we know ourselves if we do not know God? The real understanding of ourselves is our understanding of God.

PERSIAN WISDOM

13 OCTOBER

So strong is our desire to have things our own way, so entrenched is the need to control, so fearful are we of taking risks, that we need daily meditation to learn how to be gentle and sensitive, to wait and be still, to notice things and begin to believe not just that it is safe to trust but that our only hope is to allow God to take control.

Some of us have a blind hardness that quickly surfaces when our patch is threatened. It is the gift of prayer that softens our hardened hearts.

Mine, O thou lord of life, send my roots rain.

GERALD MANLEY HOPKINS

Week 42

Noticing the smallest changes in nature helps us to relish life afresh each day.

14 OCTOBER

When I was a student, I spent three months in New York, working in a child and adolescent therapy centre in a very poor, black district. Families were seen by the psychiatrist, the psychologist and the social worker and a plan was worked out with them. The area where our clients lived was dangerous, but I decided, not without some fears, to visit it on my own. There I met some of the warmest, most welcoming families I have ever known. I saw poverty and desperate efforts to provide food, clothes, education and work for the children. The people had developed a thrift shop, a play group, a club, a library, a ballet group and a civil rights group without any support from anyone. Many of the local people had never heard of the clinic. Those who had, had been referred and were afraid that if they refused to attend their child might be taken from them. Attendance cost half of their weekly income.

I did regret my visits to this neighbourhood – I regretted that I hadn't followed my heart and gone three months earlier.

A longing fulfilled is sweet to the soul.

PROVERBS 13:19

15 OCTOBER

When we dare to see with the eyes of the soul, we begin to see sharper images, things seem closer to us, our intuitive powers grow. We develop an ability to grasp and understand the unseen or non-rational elements of the world. To see with the soul is to see with our whole self. This is an intentional, personal engagement, an act of spiritual intimacy, the most profound interaction with the world that most of us have ever known.

As we allow images to enter and move through us, there can come an experience of fierce intimacy with the world that may be a little frightening at first. But we are adaptable creatures and we can adjust to this new kind of sight.

At times my heart cries out with longing to see these things.

HELEN KELLER

16 OCTOBER

Praise is a wonderful experience. We feel marvellous when we are praised. But a little praise is enough. Just as too much criticism and nagging can affect people negatively, so also can too much praise. Too much praise can stop people taking risks, dam their creativity, and act as an impediment to growth and development.

We can wreck our present by reliving guilt from the past, by becoming so overwhelmed by yesterday's mistakes that we lock out today's joy. Equally, we can also wreck our present by our need and desire for continuous praise, assurance and affirmation.

Anyone can blame; it takes a specialist to praise.

CONSTANTIN STANISLAVSKI

17 OCTOBER

Some people seem to spend a lot of time and effort in trying to get people to notice them. For others, the opposite is the case. They'd much rather go unnoticed through the crowd.

I think the reason it does not much matter to some people whether or not they are noticed is that such people have clarified their goals, have found a way to achieve them and are able to live comfortably and peacefully with them. Even when things may not be going well, if we have come to terms with our goals we will have the freedom to see ourselves for what we are. This attitude helps to keep us humble, non-judgmental and connected to others who, like us, struggle with life, with big ideas and small realities. And so, noticed or unnoticed, we find a way to be at peace with ourselves.

And then not expecting it, you become middle-aged and anonymous. No one notices you, you achieve a wonderful freedom. It is a positive thing – you can move around unnoticed, invisible.

DORIS LESSING

18 OCTOBER

A little girl of four once said to me, 'You are an old woman.' I was fifty-nine years old, and I didn't consider myself old at all, but Emma went on, pointing to the veins in my hands, 'See those things, I don't have them. Only old people have them.' She danced around me singing, 'You are an old woman, I'm a young girl.' It wasn't that she thought of old as being a bad or sad or laughable thing to be, she was just singing to me. It was me who was having the problem, though in the end she made me laugh.

Other people can't put us in our place all by themselves, we have to go there. If we choose not to accept the role another finds for us, we need not fulfil it. That is what self-esteem is all about.

To become what we are and to become what we are capable of becoming is the only end in life.

ROBERT LOUIS STEVENSON

19 October

Living is an art. The art lies not in what we experience in life – not the notes – but in how we harmonise our experiences. In the same way that it is in music, the art of creating harmony is in the pause, in the rest between experiences. It is in those times of rest that new life is born. Those precious moments between times, after one experience stops and before another begins, are priceless, because without them life would be without focus, harmony, melody, joy or rhythm. It would be more like the grating sound of the horn or of a crow or a police car.

I am the rest between two notes.

RAINER MARIA RILKE

20 OCTOBER

It is not good to put off our dreams until tomorrow, thinking we'll start really living when the children are older and educated, when the mortgage is paid off, or when we retire. We imagine that life will be perfect in the future: that when we retire we will change totally, we will be in great shape.

But there is no 'right time' to enjoy life and there is always a right time, and that time is now. I know a woman who, at the age of forty, listed fifty dreams and made a commitment to make one dream come true each year. Today at seventy-six she has followed thirty-six of her dreams and she is a very happy, alive, free and wise woman. And she is still living a normal life, at her own pace.

We can follow her example and start living today. Every new day brings us a chance to enjoy this twenty-four hours while it's still ours.

The flower blooms for the fruit and when the fruit comes the flower withers.

KABIR

Week 43

The apple trees in autumn, heavy with fruit,
lean down offering us their gifts.

21 OCTOBER

Almost every day we have to face situations and
people we fear are more than we can handle. Often
our way of coping is to try to pass the task off to
somebody else or to leave it undone. When we feel
like this, it helps to remember that all that is expected
of us is our best. This is our time. It is not a matter
of doing great things. It is a matter of saying and
doing small things with responsibility and courage.
Nobody can do my growing for me and I should not
pass to others what is my responsibility or what I
need to experience as part of my growth process.

In the transformation and growth of all things,
every bird and feature has its proper place.

FRITJOF CAPRA

22 OCTOBER

It is hard for those of us who have always slept safely in our beds to understand what it means to be homeless, or for those of us who have always been able to walk and see and hear to understand what it is like to be unable to do so. It is impossible for people who are always in command of their lives and affairs to know what it is like to have control suddenly wrenched from their grasp.

But if we can get in touch with our own fragility we can learn to touch into the fragility of others. This is a dynamic process. If we come close to people in pain, they can call us to truth, to compassion, to competence, to centredness; they can call us to be our true selves.

. . . whatever shares
The eternal reciprocity of tears.

WILFRED OWEN

23 OCTOBER

People often have the impression that you have to be very special to work with homeless or disabled people or people who are dying, but in fact it is not like that. When we work with people who are little, broken, poor and vulnerable, who do not pretend to be strong and successful, we are challenged to look at the masks we ourselves are hiding behind. We have to let go of the masks if we are to get close to the poor. The poor teach us to be empty-handed and powerless, to allow ourselves to be touched and our hearts to open; they teach us the meaning of compassion. From them we learn that the poor and the weak are not to be discarded, rather they can lead us into a new life if we allow them.

Christ invites us not to fear prosecution because, believe me brothers and sisters, one who is committed to the poor must risk the very fate of the poor in El Salvador; we know what the fate of the poor signifies: to disappear, to be tortured, to be captive and to be found dead.

OSCAR ROMERO

24 OCTOBER

To love without judging, to forgive without seeking reward, to pledge friendship, with no strings attached – these are the signs of unconditional love. When we are loved unconditionally, we are loved for ourselves, and we feel blessed and special and chosen. And if we in turn love others unconditionally, difficult though that is, then our own spirit becomes truly rich and generous and we come to learn that we can only keep what we give away and that everything we send out comes back to us.

Love is patient, love is kind. It does not envy, it does not boast, it is not proud. It is not rude, it is not self-seeking, it is not easily angered, it keeps no record of wrongs. Love does not delight in evil but rejoices with the truth. It always protects, always trusts, always hopes, always perseveres.

1 CORINTHIANS 13:4–7

25 OCTOBER

I knew a woman who, after her husband's sudden death, lost everything. Suddenly she had no home, no job, no income. She described the feeling to me: 'When I walk down the street I feel so ashamed, I feel as though I have a neon light over my head saying homeless.' For her it was a devastating experience to have that label put on her. Fortunately, she has since been able to make a new home for herself and her family.

We do tremendous harm by putting labels on people. People who have no job, no family, no friends, no home, no address, have taught me this. They have also taught me how easy it is to define ourselves by what we do and what we have rather than by who we are. But it is what we *are* that counts, and striving to realise that is the work of a lifetime.

If you shut your door
To all errors truth
Will be shut out.

RABINDRANATH TAGORE

26 OCTOBER

We all play different roles in life and often we seem to be different people in different situations, depending on the role we are playing. But if we allow ourselves to be defined by our roles, we can easily lose touch with our true selves. When the images we present in different situations are in conflict, confusion can arise for ourselves and for others.

To prevent this happening, we need to make a conscious effort to be our true selves in every situation. We need to make the different parts of ourselves and the different images we present come together and become integrated. The greater acceptance we have of who we are, the less we need to deny any part of ourselves, and the more at home and comfortable with ourselves we become.

To know what you prefer, instead of humbly saying amen to what the world tells you you ought to prefer, is to keep your soul alive.

ROBERT LOUIS STEVENSON

27 OCTOBER

Moral imagination is the special gift of the prophet and the artist. The artist listens and looks attentively and sees and hears the pain and suffering of the world, and it is from these experiences that the artist creates new images. Without moral imagination there is no compassion, for it is from the ability to picture the suffering of others that we develop the skill to imagine other ways of living.

Solutions to political problems depend on moral imagination. We find these solutions in the process of being and doing, listening and seeing, with deep sensitivity, to the insights of our imagination. But it is not just artists who exercise their imagination in this way: we are all called to sensitise our perception so that we come to learn where real suffering and injustice lie.

We are not always able to feel the love we would like to feel. But we may behave imaginatively, envisioning and eventually creating what is not present. This is what I call moral imagination.

M C RICHARDS

The fruit contains the seed and the seed contains the fruit. What we harvest in this season provides the seed for the next season.

28 OCTOBER

When I was a child, we had patchwork quilts on our beds that my mother made out of scraps of cloth. I always loved those quilts, and it seems to me that patchwork quilts are a perfect image of the potential of things that can easily be overlooked. Scraps of cloth that would otherwise be discarded, when sewn together into patterns draw beauty from each other, a beauty that was not evident before.

The same thing can happen with people. A poor, uneducated or apparently insignificant person can easily be ignored, cast aside and excluded, but if this person is placed with somebody who believes in them, their own special beauty and gifts can shine out.

But when the sun of awareness shines on the river of our perceptions the mind is transformed. Both river and sun are of the same nature.

THICH NHAT HANH

29 OCTOBER

'Oh, I couldn't do that. That is for people who have a gift for it.' We all say things like this. But if we stop to ask ourselves why we do not want to be involved, we often find that it isn't really that we lack the talent but that we don't know the talents we've got. We may know the talent we have developed, and we assume that's all there is. I find it is sometimes useful to feel inadequate to a task, because it makes me stop and examine why it is that I feel I cannot do it. Sometimes, in a situation where I would not have thought it possible to cope, I find that if I say, 'Here I am, God, I will do it with you, I will go there with you,' then I *can* cope. We are only called by the spirit to do what is suited to our gifts, even if it doesn't seem that way in the beginning. The world is as good as the many talents and gifts we commit ourselves to discovering, developing and offering.

We cannot take any credit for our talents. It is how we use our talents that counts.

MADELEINE L'ENGLE

30 October

Sometimes we feel burdened and oppressed by other people. They need us, they weigh on us. We think that if only they would leave us alone we could realise our potential. At other times we feel desperately isolated and alone, wishing we had someone we could call on and depend on. If someone cared, we think, we would be happy and could realise our potential.

The truth is we need both our independence and our interdependence. We need others, but we also need to be alone. True freedom is found when we recognise and accept our need both for unity and for separateness.

There is no light without shadow and no psychic wholeness without imperfection.

CARL GUSTAV JUNG

31 OCTOBER

All things seem possible to us when we are young. All the world's problems look solvable. It all seems so simple to us as children – if people would just love each other.

As we grow older we discover the complexities of the world and learn something we did not know as a child – that everything in the world is interrelated and interconnected, and that if we are to change any of those features we thought of as problems we have to be prepared for everything to change, for good or for ill.

As we grow older, we need to hold on to the hope, the vision, the enthusiasm of childhood. We can't solve the world's problems, but we need to believe that by changing even one thing for the good of another, we are in fact affecting every other part of the world in a way that we cannot comprehend.

When we try to pick out anything by itself, we find it hitched to everything else in the universe.

JOHN MUIR

November/December

As we gather our year together, we are grateful *for what we have been given and we* remember *what has passed.*

These months are a time to remember those who have gone before us and to remember our own past. This is also a time to let go of what has been and is being taken from us.

As we enter again into the darkness and barrenness of winter, we gather together the whole year, twelve months of joys and sorrows, hopes and fears, loves and dreams. We embrace our garden which has been made more authentic, more beautiful, more creative through the year, and give thanks for it.

1 NOVEMBER

As we enter the winter, we come to the Sabbath time of the year, when nature rests. In our anxiety to go places and do things in our busy lives, we miss things in the world about us and lose opportunities for grace. A sense of Sabbath, a commitment to taking time and space out of our busy lives and giving it to the sacred, can restore our openness to grace and make us alive to the miracles around us.

There is nothing so much like God in all the universe as silence.

MEISTER ECKHART

2 NOVEMBER

The childhood experiences we remember tend to be the disagreeable ones. We can remember being taught to sit up straight, not to speak with our mouth full, not to pick our nose, not to sneeze or cough without putting our hands over our mouth and excusing ourselves. These are all things we have to learn, of course, in order to grow from our personal to our social selves, but this can be a delicate and painful transition. Our attitude to our creativity and our sense of self-worth and self-esteem are directly connected with our early socialisation and memories.

That is why it is important also to remember, quite deliberately, the pleasures of childhood: squelching in the mud; rolling in the hay; falling into bog holes; splashing in and out of streams, river and sea; running with the wind.

Such good things can happen to people who learn to remember.

EMILY DICKINSON

3 NOVEMBER

Jesus said to his disciples: 'Why do you see the speck in your neighbour's eye, but do not notice the log in your own eye?'

The reason we cannot find good in others is that we are so blinded by our own faults. If the window in our kitchen is dirty we will see the washing on our neighbour's line as less than clean. The way to clean our window – clear our vision – is to be aware of the limitations of our vision and simply refuse to pick out the weakness in others but concentrate instead on the good.

He has the right to criticise who has the heart to help.

ABRAHAM LINCOLN

Week 45

Dying leaves can make us forget the joy they gave us when they were fresh and green.

4 NOVEMBER

Everyone by now knows the metaphor of roots and wings: we give our children roots so that they know who they are and have a sense of their own uniqueness and their place in the world; and we give them wings so that they can take responsibility for their own lives, for their emotions and attitudes and for their contribution to society.

We all need both roots and wings, but our life may be a continuous struggle between our roots and our wings, our desire to stay put and be productive and grow, and our desire to dream of other possibilities and fly off to achieve that dream. In resolving that struggle we can become both more rooted and more free to move out.

When you love someone you have to let them go. It is the only way to keep them.

MACRINA WIEDERKEHR

5 NOVEMBER

I grew up beside a river, which I thought was very deep. I spent long hours attempting to cross it by stepping from one rock to another. When I was perched on a rock I felt safe, but the satisfaction of safety soon wore off and I sought the challenge of stepping on to the next rock. That moment between two rocks was always scary, but it was that insecure, challenging, scary moment that made the whole endeavour so thrilling. It is a willingness to take the risk, to meet the challenge, to leap to the next rock that moves us from the safety of our rigid way of life into a new vision and a new life. Insecurity is painful, but sometimes we must give ourselves over to it, if we are to move on and achieve maturity.

It's we who breathe, in, out, in the sacred
Leaves astir, our wings
Rising, ruffled, but only the saints
take flight. We cower
in cliff crevice or edge-out gingerly
On branches close to the nest.

DENISE LEVERTOV

6 NOVEMBER

A place is a piece of the environment that has been claimed by feelings. Most of us love to travel and see many places, but there is no place like the place you truly know and love because you have lived there all your life. We are homesick for *places*, their sights and sounds and smells, not for environments.

If we allow our place to speak to us we will know what it is offering, but if we don't do this we will simply be visiting, like people on a tour.

Nothing can cure the soul but the senses,
just as nothing can cure the senses but the soul.

OSCAR WILDE

7 NOVEMBER

Children are naturally playful. In fact, their ability to take playfulness seriously is what marks them out as different from adults. The precious gift of childhood is freedom from the need to succeed at everything. Children enjoy the experience of going down the slide, splashing in the water, swinging on the swing, rather than their success at these activities.

We adults, on the other hand, can become so frightened of failure that we are paralysed, unable to create anything for fear of looking foolish. One way for adults to shake off that adult concern with success and to recapture their childhood joy in creation is to become involved in painting or drawing or any art form.

He who knows others is wise, he who knows himself is enlightened.

LAO TZU

8 NOVEMBER

For years, centuries, religious and church institutions believed they had all the truth and all the answers. But the spiritual way is the way of the pilgrim and the way of the pilgrim is the way of continuous renewal, a way where there is no destination, only journeying, no answers, only questing.

Arrogance dies slowly, but the way of the pilgrim is the way of humility, acknowledging that we have been and can be wrong. We can *think* that we are holy, we can *think* that we have the truth. We can *think* that we are different. We can *think* that we can judge others. But if we do, then we are unconsciously Pharisees.

When all the love of the I and the Mine is dead, then the work of the Lord is done.

KABIR

9 NOVEMBER

What is it about life that compels us to look in the places of the dead? Why do tombs and graveyards exert such a magnetic attraction for us, so that we feel compelled to visit the graves of dead friends and relatives or the tombs of the mighty?

I believe we visit places of the dead because we know that we are 'in-between' people, who exist in the now of time, and at the same time in the not yet of the final coming. We are always in the now and on the way, and we know somewhere in us that we are an Easter people, a people with hope even in darkness and suffering. We know instinctively that death and life are one and that death does not mean separation of the spirit. Rather it is a unity of the spirits in some mysterious way. The dead are closer to us in spirit than they were when they were alive.

Between two worlds life hovers like a star,
'Twixt night and morn, upon the horizons verge.
How little do we know that which we are!

LORD BYRON

10 NOVEMBER

At a seminar on leadership recently, with leaders in social, economic and spiritual fields from different parts of the world, I listened to an address given by a world-renowned expert. As time went by, though his words were resonant, I felt I was hearing nothing new. I took my courage into my hands and said so. There was a deafening silence and then he said calmly, 'Yes, that is exactly it. You know all these basic eternal concepts already because they are eternal truths. What is important is that we can claim and proclaim them.' To get in touch with these eternal truths within us we need to simplify and empty our minds and transform our inner spiritual nourishment into the strength we need. The road to spiritual growth is different for everyone, but it is essential for everyone. It does not matter how we get on the path to the eternal truths that are waiting for us, as long as we make the journey.

The light of love is like a morning star
Which lives in the heart of everyone.

INDIAN WISDOM

Week 46

The dormant buds of winter remind us of our finiteness and of our infinite possibilities.

11 NOVEMBER

My father was a farmer and all summer he lived in fear that the good weather would not hold out for long enough so that we could save the hay. But I remember that atmosphere of fear and anxiety only very vaguely. What I remember with great clarity about my childhood summers is the smell of the new-mown hay, and helping my father to turn the hay after it had been cut so that it would dry out thoroughly.

My good memories are stronger, but I do not deny the fearful memories: in remembering what was fearful I also learn. When I learn to replace denial with acceptance, I begin to see life whole and come to understand that the shadows and the dark places of my life add to the beauty of the whole, because without the darkness and the shadows the brightness would not be bright.

Fair seed-time had my soul, and I grew up
Fostered alike by beauty and by fear.

WILLIAM WORDSWORTH

12 NOVEMBER

Memories are important, but there is, too, a wisdom in forgetting, in distancing ourselves from the sadnesses of the past. There are times when we are simply not strong enough to deal with our memories and so they wait for us to grow stronger – some instinctive knowing within us honours that fear. When we are ready to remember, reminders will come in little ways, and within those reminders will come the necessary strength for remembrance.

Once you make a decision, the universe conspires to make it happen.

RALPH WALDO EMERSON

13 NOVEMBER

Where I come from is a village called Rinn Buí, which means the yellow mound. It was called that because so many daffodils grew in that area, and one particular field, which belonged to a woman in the village, turned completely yellow with daffodils in the early spring. This field of daffodils was for me a field of love and beauty, a sanctuary, a place of comfort, a place of peace. It was a place where energy came from, and I would sit on a wall beside the field and gaze at it.

I didn't have words to describe what I felt then, but years later, looking back I can see that a divine energy was coming to me from that piece of earth, and because I had an openness to it as a child, I was being blessed by it, and was able to carry that memory with me for the rest of my life. I have allowed that memory to heal me at times, now that I live in the greyness of the inner city.

Remember this, that very little is needed to make a happy life.

MARCUS AURELIUS

14 NOVEMBER

In our unconscious we remember everything. We remember the wonder and the fears of our childhood, the beauty of our environment, the sunrises and the sunsets, the yearnings of our hearts and our loneliness. I remember as a child rising very early, working round the farm, doing jobs, watching the cows being milked, calves being fed, the cocks crowing, the ducks going straight to the river, the hens cackling – and these memories are so strong in me that I still love the morning time best of all.

To enter into our memories, we need time. We need time and solitude to ask ourselves what treasures are hidden in our memories, and we need to listen to what comes.

The space between events is where most of life is lived, those half remembered moments of joy or sadness, fear or disappointment are merely beads of life strung together to make one expanding necklace of experience.

NANCY WOODS

15 NOVEMBER

Sometimes our pain is severe, sometimes not. It can consist of small daily obstacles and irritations, or it can be in the form of troubles that go on and on, with constant mental or physical pain, depression, negativity and frustration. Whatever the difficulties that we experience, they can be a source of spiritual growth. So much depends on how we view our pain and how we use it. Pain received rightly has the power to transform our lives.

What would happen if we met our troubles, our pains and our heartaches as we would meet a visitor having something to teach us. What if we stayed with our pain and asked it to help us?

'Our Kingdom go' is the necessary and unavoidable corollary of 'Thy Kingdom come'. For the more there is of self the less there is of God.

A HUXLEY

16 NOVEMBER

Some people are called to undergo the most unspeakable sufferings, whether by natural disaster, by disease or by being brutalised by society. The people of Auschwitz, the forgotten people in Romania, Somalia, Cambodia, Angola, Algeria, Rwanda, Kosovo, Northern Ireland, Calcutta and Honduras.

People who have suffered greatly have much to teach us. Every day in our lives when we meet people who are rejected by society – homeless people, prisoners, people in mental hospitals, people who are depressed, people who have been abandoned – we are meeting beautiful people, if only we can see beyond their suffering.

The mind is its own place and in it self
Can make a Heav'n of Hell and a Hell of Heav'n.

JOHN MILTON

17 November

When my great friend and mentor, Bishop Birch, died suddenly in 1981, I experienced a devastating shock and an immense sense of loss such as I had never experienced before. It took me a long time to discover that God was leading me into another dimension of my life, into knowing God in a new way. When I fell ill myself in 1990, I experienced a great sense of powerlessness. And yet that suffering, in a mysterious way was an occasion for an encounter with God that was both terrifying and supremely wonderful, for God showed himself to me as the God of love. None of us wants to experience suffering, but it comes our way, and when it does it has its own way of breathing new life. If we can stay with it and find our true selves in it, we will discover that we can grow through it to our full stature.

In order to arrive there,
To arrive where you are, to get from where you
   are not,
You must go by a way wherein there is no ecstasy.

T S ELIOT

Week 47

The bare branches covered in snow remind us that there is beauty in our less than perfect selves.

18 NOVEMBER

Great people who have endured great suffering don't boast about their suffering but rather use it as a source of hope for others. Not only was Jesus hurt and abused in death, but he was hurt and humiliated in life. People around him challenged his message, stopped his mission and eventually took his life away. His life was interrupted, cut off, at a young age. Though he was so loving and kind, he had a tremendously violent death. How did he live it all out with such integrity and dignity? How do other people do it? I believe they do it because they live out of an inner strength and wisdom. Some call that spirit, or God, or some other name, but we all know it is a force stronger than ourselves, a force that calls forth the best in us and inspires us.

Our deepest fear is not that we are inadequate, our deepest fear is that we are powerful beyond measure. You are a child of God. We are born to manifest the glory of God that is within us. It is not just in some of us, it is in everyone.

NELSON MANDELA

19 NOVEMBER

Gathering together our personal stories and naming and claiming our past is critical for all of us, because knowing where we have come from helps us to know where we are going. This applies not just to individuals but also to families, to communities and to organisations.

It is also critical for cultures and nations to recall their history, their suffering, poverty, famines and what it was that brought them through it. Especially in times of oppression and hardship, it is often a country's poets and writers who tell the stories, bear witness and hoard the memories of the people for the future.

Remembering is about wallowing in the past: it is about enabling us to live more fully in the present and for leading us into the future.

Many poets did not survive but their works remain with us as a poetic witness, to the dark times in which they and we lived.

CAROLYN FORCHÉ

20 NOVEMBER

Memories expand boundaries.

When my mother was old, she would vividly recall the visits of people from the Blasket islands, which appeared to her to have happened just a few hours earlier, or even as she told them, but which had in fact happened eighty years before.

But even though she was confused about the present, her memory was clear. With memory there are no real losses in life. We can store everything away in our memory storerooms, where we carry everything and everyone we ever encountered, and we can visit them again and again. We can all be children, adolescents, young people again. Memories are like diamonds, sunlit. With our memories we need never be lonely.

Only be careful, and watch yourself closely so that you do not forget the things your eyes have seen or let them slip from your heart as long as you live. Teach them to your children and to their children after them.

DEUTERONOMY 4:9

21 NOVEMBER

Many people think of prayer as an activity to be added to their daily tasks, but prayer is not to be confused with saying prayers. If we see prayer as wholehearted living it is easier to recognise prayer as an attitude that characterises all our activities.

The more we come alive and awake, the more everything we do becomes prayer. If prayerfulness is our highest degree of aliveness, the starting point must be whenever and wherever we are most alive. That may be when we recite a psalm, when we eat or drink, or when we walk with openness and wonderment. What matters is prayer, not prayers.

Yet prayers also have their place. They fulfil our need to express our prayerfulness.

The still mind of a sage is a mirror of heaven and earth, the glass of all things.

CHAUNG TZU

22 NOVEMBER

Mary Aikenhead, the founder of my congregation, the Irish Sisters of Charity, established a vibrant, dedicated congregation – in a time of famine, disease and cholera – to respond to the needs of the poor. She wrote hundreds of letters which give us insight into what life in Ireland was like in the early nineteenth century and which reveal the spirit, the self-sacrifice and dedication, and her love for the poor in the midst of desperate suffering. Had she never written these letters, her work would still have been valid, but so much would have been lost that we as a congregation would be less able to understand who we are, where we have come from and what we are called to.

What a miracle it is that out of these
small flat, rigid squares of paper,
unfolds world after world after world.
Worlds that sing to you,
comfort and quiet or excite you.
Books help us to understand who we are and how
we are to behave.

ANNE LAMOTT

23 NOVEMBER

A woman once described her relationship with her mother in these words: 'I can still hear her scolding me from her grave.'

Some people are left all their life burdened with uncertainty and frustration because they are still held by negative messages from their parents. Others carry through their lives a false sense of loyalty to their parents.

We all – even those of us who have positive relationships with our parents – need to free ourselves from our emotional dependence on our parents if we are to grow into maturity. We need to break ties that are burdensome if we are to realise our full potential.

It is only when we have learnt to see our parents for who they were and when we have ceased to expect the impossible of them that we can begin to learn the important task of parenting our own children in a way that enables them to grow into maturity and enables us to let them go.

When we cling to pain we end up punishing ourselves.

LEO F BUSCAGLIA

24 November

Our resistance to pain can lead us to insulate ourselves against suffering. Sometimes, when we open our hearts to the suffering of others, our reaction is to close down again quickly, because we are so frightened, and we substitute denial for the natural outpouring of our hearts.

But pain stretches us, pushes us to grow and develop, and we can only be healers to each other if we have shared the experience of pain. We can only be present to another's suffering and sorrow if we have first acknowledged and embraced our own pain.

The wounded healer is the true healer. Those who cannot acknowledge or accept their own pains and wounds can neither heal nor be healed.

Nothing can work the damage except myself
I am a real sufferer by my fault.

ST BERNARD OF CLAIRVAUX

Week 48

The harmony and balance that we find in the outdoor world is the perfect antidote to the materialism of Christmas. Nature opens our mind but never overloads it.

25 NOVEMBER

Very little of true worth is attained without pain. Whether our pain consists of illness, physical or mental, opposition from others or the struggle to make difficult decisions, no growth is achieved without it.

When pain emerges, our tendency is to draw back. But if we stay with the pain, we can discover that it brings us to new solutions. If we avoid the pain, there is a real danger we will stay with the old situation and not find the solutions.

The challenge is to look at the pain and see it clearly. That is the only way we can see the possibilities within it, and then slowly move with it, into what it is calling us to. And no matter how slow the journey may be, if we are true to ourselves and to our pain, we will be led to growth and to peace.

Life is of the soul and of nothing else . . .
Love and laughter ride with it, but so do pain and anguish.

KEN WILBER

26 NOVEMBER

The story of Genesis tells us that God created not just the world and all that is in it, but also rest; and he commanded us to take rest. The Jewish religion teaches that the Sabbath equalises the rich and the poor, because for at least one day the rich and the poor are equally free from the constrains of work. Also, the Sabbath provides time to evaluate work, as Yahweh evaluated the work of creation, to determine whether our work, like God's, is good. And, finally, the purpose of the Sabbath is to give us some time to contemplate the meaning of life.

Today the Sabbath is more important than ever, because we in this society are in danger of over-working ourselves into illness.

If the sould could have known God without the world, the world would have never been created.

MEISTER ECKHART

27 NOVEMBER

Last year, during a retreat I was giving (on the theme of hope) to a group of priests, I asked if they would spend some time looking for a symbol that meant hope to them. They came up with an extraordinary variety of symbols: symbols of light, symbols of nature and the earth, something they themselves had created. What was interesting was that when they explained why they had chosen particular things, they nearly all associated their symbol with a memory, and so their symbols of hope about the future were symbols that carried meaning about the past. They were remembering moments of joy, and hope came back to them after long absences.

The unstruck drum of Eternity is sounded within me; but my deaf ears cannot hear it.

KABIR

28 NOVEMBER

'Behold, I have made all things new,' God tells us, and indeed the cosmos is constantly renewing itself and constantly giving rise to forms that never existed before. And the most exciting thing about this novelty is that it is unpredictable.

For some people, unpredictability is scary, but in fact being prepared not to know is a true recognition that there is a power higher than ourselves. If we are prepared to experience what life has to offer, we have to be prepared for unpredictability. Then, not knowing what will happen becomes for us not a deficiency but a source of creativity and a way to sense the divine.

Darkness is more productive of sublime ideas than light.

EDMUND BURKE

29 NOVEMBER

In silence a flower blooms, in silence it fades away.
   There is a place in the depth of our being that is protected and saved for ourselves, an inner, sacred space guarded by God's presence. It is up to each one of us to find that place. Sometimes we only howl into it when we are broken or wounded and empty, but it is in and through that emptiness that we can find our way into the beauty that transforms us into strong, loving, wise and beautiful people.

You shall have joy or you shall have power, you shall not have both.

RALPH WALDO EMERSON

30 NOVEMBER

When we become less preoccupied with doing things and more with being, when we are less attentive to making decisions and more able to let our desires well up into our consciousness, when we are less attentive to our reason and logic and more attentive to our intuition, when we are less focused on why we are unable to do something and more attentive to what we are doing, then we discover our enormous resources and creativity.

When we are less concerned with searching for God and more aware of all the places God finds us in our daily lives, then we begin to assume a willing attitude towards life and we become open, receptive and respectful, rather than dominating and grasping.

What the caterpillar calls the end of life, the master calls a butterfly.

R BLACK

1 DECEMBER

Children have a need and an ability to become totally absorbed in what they are doing, and also just to stand and look for a long time. But often adults come along and pull the children out of their wonderment, out of their *kairos* time, reminding them they have no more time. And the long arm pulls the little child along.

No wonder that by the time we are adults we have lost that ability to stop and stare; no wonder that our sense of mystery is lost to us. Children take the time to look and to live in the now, and we have to try to do the same. It's never too late to recover our sense of the now, because it is as natural to us as breathing, and the child within us never loses the ability to look with the eyes of the heart, combining concentration with wonderment.

A well-educated child ought to be able to sit and look when nothing is to be seen. To sit and listen when nothing is to be heard.

NATIVE AMERICAN SAYING

Week 49

Remembering beautiful things has immense healing power: enjoying the red berries of the holly, we forget the thorns.

2 DECEMBER

Resting is not passive; it is an activity with God that allows us to live our lives fully.

Our everyday lives can often be dulled or overwhelmed by routine and commitments, but if we take time out of the everyday to listen without distraction, we become aware of the spirit's movement within us, and we learn to develop a sense of well-being when we make right decisions. Stopping to listen can help us to recognise God within the complexity of our lives. It can also help us when the rhythm of our life shifts and we face new personal, social or spiritual challenges and opportunities.

Within this earthen vessel are bowers and groves and within it is the creator.

KABIR

3 DECEMBER

The Latin tradition defines peace as *tranquillitas ordinis*, the stillness of order. It is not a static but a dynamic stillness. It is the candle lighting, the flame burning, moving, but in a calm and orderly way so that to gaze on it stills us. A spinning wheel is the same: it whirls at great speed but about a still centre; similarly, a river is eternally flowing but is nevertheless in the same place. Any of these experiences – contemplating a candle burning steadily, watching a wheel, listening to the river – can help us to enter into our own place of inner peace, where we can find and be at one with ourselves.

. . . music heard so deeply
That it is not heard at all, but you are the music
While the music lasts.

T S ELIOT

4 DECEMBER

Most people will have some experience of depression, whether brought on by distress, pain or loss or caused by an inner darkness. Depression is like taking a lonely walk down a long, long corridor, to a door at the end that turns out to be closed.

As we approach that last, locked door, we need to be reminded that all along the corridor are other doors. These doors are people who are with us in our distress.

Depression speaks in absolutes, telling us there is no way out, no relief from the hurt, and that feeling can paralyse us. Yet we know also that this isn't true, that there are ways out – professional help is available if we need it and those who love us can also help, reaching out to us in love. Sometimes, we are just too depressed to look for the ways out.

But no one needs to walk alone. That is a thought that we must hold fast to on the darkest days.

When you see a man in distress, recognise him as a fellow man.

SENECA

5 DECEMBER

Choices and decisions are much simpler and easier to make if we learn to listen to our inner voice. By tuning in to what we really feel, we can come to know the sound and feel of right and wrong and out of that make clear decisions. When we're on the track that is right for us, we experience a sense of 'Ah, yes! That's right for me.' When we try to force an unhealthy choice we get lost and our pathway is confused and dark. We may have felt or known all along this or that wasn't the right way, but we were moving out of fear or denial or pressure, and we were unable to see clearly.

There are no perfect decisions. Life is never crystal clear. All of us at one time or another regret a decision or a choice we've made. But when we rely on our heart and reflect on our sense of right and wrong and think less about what others would think of us or what they would choose, then we are free to make good decisions, ones that are right for us.

The seeming truth which cunning times put on
To entrap the wisest.

WILLIAM SHAKESPEARE

6 DECEMBER

People are tiring of the competitive, consumer-driven world we live in. They are starting to ask, What can be done to reverse the trend towards extreme individualism? How can we live our lives, caring for ourselves and being supportive to others?

I believe that we can only fill this gap by developing a sense of ownership of the world and times we live in. This is our time and it is up to us to choose our destinies. What happens here, now, is our responsibility. It is not a matter of doing great things: it is a matter of doing or saying small things with responsibility and courage.

There is only the fight to recover what has been
    lost
And found and lost again and again . . .
But perhaps neither gain nor loss.
For us, there is only the trying. The rest is not
    our business.

T S ELIOT

7 DECEMBER

How we perceive people and things affects our attitudes; our attitudes affect our response; our response affects the people and situations we come into contact with, and so it goes on.

If we perceive the homeless as people who drink, who don't want to work or help themselves, then our attitude to them is that they don't deserve a lot of help and we simply provide food, clothes and shelter for them; that in turn affects their perception of themselves and gradually it seeps into their psyche that they are not worth much. If, on the other hand, we treat them as people who happen to be down on their luck and who have all kinds of potential within them, like all of us, then our response to them will be quite different, and that positive response will in turn help them to realise their own possibilities.

And now here is my secret, a very simple secret. It is only with the heart that one can see rightly; what is essential is invisible to the eye.

ANTOINE DE SAINT-EXUPÉRY

8 DECEMBER

Where I come from, in Dingle on the southwest coast of Ireland, we never say that someone has died, but that they are gone on the way of truth – *imithe ar slí na fírinne*. This is not to deny death, but to see it as part of the natural cycle of life. All living and growing things are part of a cycle of endings and beginnings, planting and harvesting. Our fear of death is a resistance to that natural order and flow of life. We forget our place in a bigger picture and view death as an unnatural event, which robs us of our joy in living. Dr Elisabeth Kübler-Ross speaks of death as a natural transition into beauty and harmony. She believes that death is really a birthday, that death is merely a doorway into a love-filled tomorrow. We walk to the door when the time is right, and it will open for us into peace beyond our understanding.

Sleepe after toyle, port after stormy seas,
Ease after warre, death after life doth greatly
    please.

EDMUND SPENCER

Week 50

We discover summer in winter when we take the time to develop our capacity and readiness to do so.

9 DECEMBER

Our inner beauty flows through our eyes, our smiles, our expression, our gestures, our peacefulness, our warmth, our joy, our concern. We stultify our own beauty by trying to model ourselves on the images that are set for us by others about the way we think we should look, the way we should feel, the way we should dress, walk and talk. Instead of being dissatisfied ourselves, we will be more joyful if we honour the sacred garment that is given to us for our journey, a garment that is beautiful and a work of art.

What you want is profoundly expensive
And difficult to find,
Yet close by.

LALLA

10 December

To let go with grace is to challenge one of our deepest instincts – self-preservation. It is not easy to live with ambiguity. We all crave certainty; we have developed our capacity to know to the point that we are very uncomfortable with not knowing. In letting go, there is usually a clearly identifiable moment of loneliness, doubt and risk before the point of realisation happens. But when the waiting is endured without recourse to distractions, when the emptiness is sustained without reaching for fillers, then we can be transformed, because it is in that emptiness and darkness and brokenness that greatness is found. The darkness is like a womb waiting. There is a purification of consciousness, as the stressful breaking-free from familiar perimeters happens and as an exhilarating openness to ever-new possibilities is born. Letting go is darkness emptying, waiting, dying and birthing. It is in the letting go that new life begins.

Self inside self, you are nothing but me.
Self inside self, I am only you.

LALLA

11 DECEMBER

Deep in most of us there is the desire for liberation
from the forces that stifle us. The grace of letting go
needs to be at the heart of all our passions. Acknowledging and accepting our brokenness is a kind of
dying. Letting go is like dying into freedom, like
sinking beneath the waves only to find a new security.

It seems that we have two fundamental forces
within us, the law of fear which leads to distrust and
the law of love, whose essence is to let go, to give
way, to act positively, by trusting, creating, healing,
emptying and surprising. The law of love teaches us
a strange truth: that all we give away is given back
to us, that what we give ourselves increases the love
that we have. We can only take with us when we
die what we let go of when we were alive.

Inside you there is an artist you don't know about.

RUMI

12 December

Our pain and our wounds are as much part of our humanity as our joy and wholeness. It is never easy to reach out to embrace our wounds, but once we do the wounds are transformed.

The medieval mystics wrote of the importance of darkness. They identify silence, suffering and pain as the way to finding our true selves. Pain will transform us if we can embrace it, knowing that it will not shatter us, for we are not objects that will break, but people who have within us the power to grow to our full capacity.

Do you think you shall enter the garden of bliss without such trials as came to those who have passed before you?

THE KORAN

13 DECEMBER

The model that Christians are given for living our lives is the life of Jesus. He risked everything; he was abandoned, rejected, betrayed and killed for being who he was. He was crucified for asking the right questions of the right people and for standing up and taking responsibility for the right things.

This is not an easy model to live up to, but if we are willing to live with honesty and integrity, letting go of falsity, we will attain a sense of freedom and truth. Once we break through the pretences, the barriers, the falsities that blind us and bind us, we will be free for ever, and no one will ever take that freedom from us.

A condition of complete simplicity
(costing not less than everything)
And all shall be well . . .

T S ELIOT

14 December

We seem to have learnt that our aim must be to be full. And yet it is only when we make space that we can be loved, and it is only across space that encouragement comes. It is only when we are open and empty that we can be empowered to believe in ourselves and to explore the richness and beauty within us. It is only when we are empty and make space that we can be healed of those false fears which we all have – of losing our identity, of losing our freedom.

It is much easier to give than to receive, because with giving we have a certain sense of control. But it is only when we have learnt to receive, to be open and empty, that we will get gifts such as understanding, appreciation of our friends and loved ones, the ability to look anew at people and things that we may have taken for granted, and a sense of gratitude for everything we have been given.

I make myself rich by making my words few.

HENRY DAVID THOREAU

15 December

Exploring is exciting but it is also scary. When we explore we leave our places of safety and comfort and move into the unknown. Our inward journey may not be as dramatic as the journeys of the great explorers but it is still an exploration, because it is a moving away to face the unknown. When we face our demons and acknowledge our weakness and our frailty, we discover extraordinary gifts. When we move from our comfort zones to walk the authentic path, we marvel at the unimagined jewels of beauty and truth we discover in our inner, unknown continent.

So here I am, in the middle way having had twenty
  years –
Twenty years largely wasted, the years of *l'entre
  deux guerres* –
Trying to learn to use words, and every
  attempt
Is a wholly new start, and a different kind of
  failure.

T S ELIOT

Week 51

Our Christmas tree is an expression of joy in ourselves and in our world.

16 December

Living today is a challenge, a risk and an act of trust. Most of us grew up learning unconsciously that planning was part of life. At school we learnt that the more prepared we were for exams, the better we would perform.

All that is true, but it is also true that we can live the here and now, and if we do live today fully it prepares us for tomorrow. It takes courage to fully experience this day, this love, instead of regretting yesterday and planning tomorrow.

To live fully now means we must trust it will be enough, because we are exactly where we are meant to be at this time. Living in today makes us vulnerable, but it also brings peace and serenity. When we surrender tomorrow in order to live today, we are happier and freer.

Every day, no matter how bad it may be, I shall say from tomorrow on I shall be sad, not today.

CHILD IN A NAZI DEATH CAMP

17 December

I wore a habit for many years and when we were given permission not to wear it I was pleased. I thought getting rid of the habit would help to get rid of institutionalised attitudes, and in many ways it did. And yet, after a while, I found myself saying, 'I wish I had a uniform, life would be easier. I wouldn't have to spend time choosing clothes and making sure I have the right ones for the right occasion.'

Now I realise that if I am at home with my inner self, then that will guide my decisions about my outward appearance, and with a bit of imagination, a little can go a long way in the wardrobe department. As long as we have changes for the seasons and can dress appropriately and comfortably, then we don't need to worry too much. Over-anxiety about externals limits the expression of who we really are.

Look at this glowing day! What clothes
Could be so beautiful or
More sacred.

LALLA

18 DECEMBER

To accept ourselves completely is to accept our strengths, weaknesses, darkness and light, richness and poverty, our beauty and ugliness. It is to know ourselves and to continue on the road of discovering and knowing ourselves more deeply and freely every day. That can be terrifying

Whether we put it in a religious context or not, what we are called to do in this life is to fulfil our potential. So we must first find ourselves and not expect to find the full truth unless we continue each day to search, to seek what we are being called to. This is the struggle of a lifetime.

I learn by going where I have to go.

THEODORE ROETHKE

19 DECEMBER

The sower of seed lives with hope, trusting that whatever will happen will make sense. To sow is to live with trust and conviction that go beyond the ordinary.

Human work tends to focus on producing something, but this is not always the best way to work. If the sower is focused on the end product – the harvest – then that cripples the process of surrendering to the earth, which is what sowing is about. If we don't surrender to the processes of our work, the work may appear to be successful, but it will not be truly fruitful. For our work to be fruitful, we must do it with trust, abandonment, vision and commitment.

We think eternity but we move slowly through time.

OSCAR WILDE

20 December

It is only when somebody close to us loses their sight or hearing and we imagine what it might be like not to have these senses that we begin to appreciate the wonderful gifts that hearing and vision are. Most of the time we do not use these gifts fully. We do not see all the small flowers or hear all the faint voices around us. We barely notice what there is to be seen or heard.

If we take the time to become absolutely conscious of our powers and abilities we can experience the wonder of listening and seeing. If we look and listen deeply and attentively and notice what it is that we are hearing and seeing, and if we take the time to listen deeply and see deeply and feel deeply with our inner ear and our inner eye and our heart, then everything will be different. It will transform our lives.

One eye sees, the other feels.

PAUL KLEE

21 DECEMBER

When a friend of mine died, I was filled with many different emotions – love, appreciation, gratitude, loneliness, emptiness, loss, sadness, frustration, anger. My friend had lived with integrity, and his death reminded me that life is about living attentively, fully and with joy. It reminded me that I have only this time now to live. All that matters is that now I am present and I know it and I know why.

The unexamined life is not worth living for a human being.

SOCRATES

22 December

I once went on a visit to Niagara Falls with a group that included several children with learning difficulties. It was a beautiful, pleasurable journey to this magnificent city thronged with tourists and sightseers, and its overwhelming waterfall. It was all delightful, but the most delightful moment was when one of the children said to me: 'It is very pretty. That is how God made the waterfall. He didn't make all the rivers like that and there is nothing that can stop the water from falling.'

This eight-year-old child with learning difficulties was able to see immediately that the waterfall was doing exactly what it was meant to do. Just as all of nature, if we allow it, does exactly what it is sent here to do, and in doing so gives beauty to all of us and glorifies the creator.

Call the world if you Please 'The vale of Soul making'
Then you will find out the use of the world.

JOHN KEATS

Week 52

We need the season of Advent to unsettle us, to challenge our priorities and intentions, to give us time to ponder, and pause.

23 DECEMBER

People often travel or make a change in their lives in order to get away from difficult situations, but changing towns, countries, jobs or partners can't change what we are. Another job, a change of scene, a new relationship – all these things can be refreshing, but they cannot work miracles.

If we feel the need to change our lives, we must be prepared to recognise that this will involve hard work, hard choices, hard decisions. Real change only comes when we make searching and painful examinations of our values and behaviour and learn from our past experiences.

When the soul wishes to experience something she throws an image of the experience out before her and enters into her own image.

MEISTER ECKHART

24 December

The beauty of the universe has immense healing power, and remembering beautiful things continues the healing.

For me, the night sky is very beautiful, especially when there is a moon. Last week I saw a blue moon, immense and very beautiful. It took me back to my childhood Christmases, when we waited outside our home to be collected by a hackney car to go to midnight mass. Every time I look at a moonlit sky it reminds me of the sheer delight of being allowed to stand out in the darkness of Christmas Eve to look at the moon. That memory is stronger for me than going to mass on Christmas night.

To me, fair friend, you never can be old;
For as you were when first your eyes I eyed,
Such seems your beauty still.

WILLIAM SHAKESPEARE

On the seventh day God rested, having created the earth. Sabbath time beats in synchronicity with the rhythms of nature.

25 DECEMBER

Those without a home feel it very deeply at Christmas. There are people who pretend they go home at this time of year rather than admit to themselves or others that they have no home to go to.

Home is the place where we discover who we are, where we are coming from and where we are going to. It is where we are helped to establish our own identity. It is where we learnt to love and be loved. It is where our needs of the mind, body and spirit are first recognised and met. It is where we learn to become whole, stable and yet always open to change and surprise.

Home is the definition of God.

EMILY DICKINSON

26 December

Wuthering Heights, a novel that went on to achieve world acclaim, was initially rejected again and again by publishers, yet its author, Emily Brontë, never lost her spirit. Just before she died at the age of thirty, she wrote about her courage and faith: 'No coward soul is mine.' Her dreams had kept her spirit light and confident against the power of fear.

Fear can easily paralyse us unless we know how to conquer it. Fear seems to come from outside, but really it comes from within ourselves, and so the real strength to combat our fear comes also from within. It comes from the spirit within us, which is a source of power and strength much greater than ourselves.

Dreams . . . they have gone through and through me, like wine through water, and altered the colour of my mind.

EMILY BRONTË

27 December

We imagine sometimes that if we can just get through this day, tomorrow will be better. The fact is, however, that we tend to follow the same patterns over and over again, so that tomorrow will be just the same as today. That is no way to live life.

I find it useful each day to plan what I need to do and in the evening to look at what I have done and not done. Looking back over a week, I can discover how I spend my days.

I began to notice patterns of behaviour which I knew I needed to change. I discovered that I constantly tried to fit too much into any one day, and then added more as the day went on. I found myself rushing from one thing to another. And even though I spend at least two hours each morning by myself in prayer and meditation, I found I needed to build in another half hour at least to be alone.

Changing my days became a challenge for me, but when I did it I found it took care of the weeks and the years.

How we spend our day is, of course, how we spend our lives.

ANNIE DILLARD

28 DECEMBER

This year I was invited to open an exhibition of sculpture by Ann McHugh, who works in copper and ceramics. The pieces were magnificent, very spiritual and yet earthy, but a particular ceramic piece stood out for me, one she had named the 'circle of life'. All forms of life were woven together to form a never-ending circle.

It is an extraordinary thing that we can neither imagine life ending nor imagine it not ending. This rich circle of life goes on; it was there before us and is here now and will continue after us. We live now, and now will soon be the past and the future now. All we have is a brief now and in now we are alone and yet we are not alone; we are accompanied in this circle, in this journey through life, by all life.

I think in order to recover what I already know, to recollect my essence, to savour the promise that has been unfolding since my birth, to see my cosmic face in the mirror of my mind.

S McNAB

29 DECEMBER

It is good and comforting, to have a daily routine, but the danger with routine is that life can become dull. To combat this we all need to be constantly renewing our lives to bring a new sense of vigour, vitality and freshness.

One way to renew our lives daily is to see life as a garden. Then we will be constantly reminded to plant new seeds, to nourish the plants and to tend them as they grow. This will ensure that our lives do not become clogged with weeds. In a garden, we know what to do to renew the soil and tend the plants, but in our lives we need to focus on living wholeheartedly in a way that transcends monotony and transforms it into vitality and creativity. In this way our lives can be constantly transformed and we will radiate freshness as we live constantly awake and constantly awakening.

We must learn to reawaken, to keep ourselves awake . . . Everyman is tasked to make his life, even in its details, worthy of the contemplation of his most elevated and most critical hour.

HENRY DAVID THOREAU

30 DECEMBER

Recently, when I went back to my homeplace, I went, as I always do, to visit my parents' grave. I found a man I knew, Pádraig, wandering through the cemetery stopping at the different graves. When I greeted him, he said, 'This is where I spend some time every week, talking to the people who have gone before me, remembering them. They're all still my friends. I speak to them all the time. I will be meeting them soon.'

Pádraig was in no way depressed or melancholy or wallowing in the past. In fact he was one of the most popular and lively men in the village. It was his closeness to life and to people that enabled him to be equally close to the dead. His remembering was his way of expressing that those who had died had not left him and he had not left them.

Truly what is stiff and hard is a companion of death, whereas what is soft and weak is a companion of life. Therefore the weapon that is too hard will be broken, the tree that has the hardest wood will be cut down.

LAO TZU

31ST DECEMBER

Each day is given to us to fulfil the purpose of our lives; we all have a unique gift and calling that is ours alone. It is an extraordinary privilege. In Isaiah we read, 'I have called you by your name, you are precious in my sight and I love you.' That is how God speaks to each of us every day if we take the time to listen. Isn't that wonderful, the sense of being called special? Being precious and unique is knowing that there is something far beyond us, watching over us. While there is much in the future and present that we cannot see or understand, that doesn't matter if we know we have a purpose in life, that gives a balance to our human situation. It is said that many people in life drift into things; school, work, marriage, having children. When we have a sense of purpose we don't drift, we listen to our call, we discern what is right at any particular time. That is something that we must do all our lives, that will bring peace and happiness.

I have brought you glory on earth by completing the work you gave me to do.

JOHN 17:4

Acknowledgements

The Publishers have used their best endeavours to contact all copyright holders. If any errors have inadvertently been made, corrections will be made in future editions.

W H AUDEN
One line from 'In Memory of W B Yeats' by W H Auden. Reprinted by kind permission of Faber & Faber Ltd and Random House, Inc.

DIETRICH BONHOEFFER
Extract from *The Cost of Discipleship* by Dietrich Bonhoeffer. Copyright ©1959 by SCM Press, Ltd. Reprinted with kind permission of SCM Press and Scribner, a division of Simon & Schuster, Inc.

W H DAVIES
Extract from *Selected Poems of W H Davies* (Jonathan Cape). Reprinted by kind permission of Mrs H M Davies.

ANNIE DILLARD
Submitted excerpts used for 30 January & 27 December entries from *Pilgrim at Tinker Creek* by Annie Dillard. Copyright © 1974 by Annie Dillard. Reprinted by permission of HarperCollins Publishers, Inc. Extracts from *Pilgrim at Tinker Creek* (Harper Perennial, 1998) by Annie Dillard. Reprinted with